MW00491786

More Voices

A Collection of Works from Asian Adoptees

Edited by Susan Soonkeum Cox

Yeong & Yeong Book Company
St. Paul, Minnesota

More Voices: A Collection of Works from Asian Adoptees

Yeong & Yeong Book Company
St. Paul, Minnesota
www.yeongandyeong.com

Interior design and typesetting: Michelle Nicolson,
                                     Black Cat Communications, LLC
Cover design: Michelle Nicolson,
                                     Black Cat Communications, LLC

Front jacket image © Kim Tobin King
Back jacket image © Jessica Emmett

Cataloging-in-Publication data is on file at the Library of Congress, http://catalog.loc.gov.

ISBN: 978-1-59743-004-3

Printed in the United States of America

15 14 13 12 11 10 1 2 3 4 5

This book is printed on acid-free paper.

To "Grandma" Bertha Holt
with love and appreciation

Contents

Introduction

Susan Soonkeum Cox

The members of the first generation of Korean adoptees were pioneers. Born in Korea to uncertain circumstances, we left the land of our birth to go to our adoptive families in the United States and Europe. We left everything behind—birth family, birth culture, birth heritage, and nationality.

For those who left Korea as infants, there were no intact memories of experiences, however brief. For children who were older, the precise losses could be remembered—at least for a time. People, language, places, food, smells—for most children adopted when they were older, the distinct memories dimmed and diminished over time. But for all of us—infant or adolescent—the connection to our adoption experience is in some measure a part of who we become as adults.

More than 200,000 of us have been adopted internationally in the past 55 years. Adoption from other countries followed the success of adoption from Korea. The humanitarian response to the Vietnam War imitated the Korean response of families wanting to adopt the children affected by war. The echo of similarity between the two wars could be seen on the faces of the many Amerasian children fathered by U.S. soldiers. Like Korea a decade before, the mixed-race children and the mothers who gave birth to them had a precarious future at best.

In addition to intercountry adoptions from Asia, countries in Latin and South America began placing children with adoptive families during the 1970s. After the fall of Ceausescu in Romania, adoptions from Eastern Europe eclipsed the number of adoptions from the rest of the world. For the first time intercountry adoption did not necessarily mean interracial adoption, and for families longing for a child that "looked like them," this seemed the perfect answer.

Adult adoptees knew differently. They had already lived the experience and understood that being the same race did not negate that children adopted from another country would have the same issues of culture, heritage, and nationality that is part of the intercountry adoption experience.

In 1999 the First International Gathering of Korean Adoptees was held in Washington, D.C. It brought together, for the first time, the pioneering generations of Korean adoptees. It was a deeply profound experience, and for many of the first generation of adoptees, it was their first time to meet other adult adoptees who were "just like me."

As part of the first Gathering, Brian Boyd of Yeong and Yeong Book Company graciously published *Voices from Another Place*, an anthology of work by Korean adoptees. *Voices from Another Place* was an opportunity to give voice to the first generation of Korean adoptees to tell their stories. The collection of essays, poetry, and art reflected the diversity of adoptees and their experiences.

It is no surprise that as adoptees we are each as individual and unique as our temperaments, beliefs, talents, and life experiences. However different adoptees are—both individually and collectively—we share the undeniable common experience of intercountry adoption. Collectively within the adult adoptee community, there is an enormous range of responses and beliefs about adoption, both personally and generally. While some adoptees consider adoption to have "given them a chance at life," there are others who feel the opposite with great passion.

More Voices: A Collection of Works from Asian Adoptees includes some of both views. It also is not just the voices of adoptees from Korea this time, but includes adoptees from other countries. It is my strong belief that although the birth country is different, many of the thoughts, feelings, joys, and challenges are the same for all international adoptees. Our commonalities are greater than our differences.

It has been 55 years since the first children from Korea came to their families through intercountry adoption. What began as the legacy of war in one country has extended to children in more than twenty countries. In the decade between *Voices from Another Place* and *More Voices: A Collection of Works from Asian Adoptees*, the Hague Convention on Intercountry Adoption has become a global treaty of understanding and commitment to ethical adoption practices that protect birth families, adoptive families, and, most of all, the children who will be adopted.

Hearing the voices of adoptees, now grown, gives us all a deeper understanding of international adoption and the families (both birth and adoptive) it touches. We raise our voices in hope that our stories will ensure that children who need families—wherever they are—will have them.

October

Joy Lieberthal

I have been in reunion with my birth mother since 1994. I was 24 years old when I learned that I was never placed for adoption by my birthmother and she had been searching for me since I left her home in 1974. I have returned to Korea many times since 1994, with tours of adoptive families, with adult Korean adoptees, and as a committee member of The Gathering of Korean Adult Adoptees. I have traveled to Korea with my Korean American husband and then again with my firstborn son. Every visit included a few hours with my birth mother and my half-brother over lunch or dinner and a little shopping. Every visit was happy, simple, and short.

Fast forward to 2009. Korea obtained the coveted "most favored nation" status and obtaining a tourist visa became a non-issue. And so, my Umma and brother came to the United States for three months. They came to stay in our one bedroom apartment that already housed my family of four. This visit challenged every cell of my brain, my heart, my patience, and my childhood fantasies of how my life could have or should have been. In the end, I made quite a lot of breakthroughs and my dear friends went along for the ride with me. Here is what I wrote about the visit as it was coming to a close...

I have read the itinerary wrong again! Because the flight is at midnight Tuesday, I kept thinking Tuesday, but it is midnight Monday night, which makes it Tuesday. Confused? Yes, me too. I was surprised with my reaction—gleeful remorse.

I have begun to tell the boys of the imminent departure of their grandma and uncle, and I am so overwhelmed with P's reaction that I had to write it down. He has been very sad and tearful and today he saw my Umma packing one of her bags. In the process of unwrapping things out of their boxes to make them fit into the suitcase, a lone paper star fell off a holiday bag. To digress for a moment, there is a tradition at our church where we sing carols during the Christmas Eve service, and during each song people go up and bring a paper ornament to decorate the naked tree up at the altar. An angel for "Hark the Herald Angels Sing," a bell for "Oh Little Town of Bethlehem"—you get the point. My favorite is the star to be hung with "Oh Holy Night." It is the sweetest song, and the music brings me to tears every time. My Umma took a star and then told me that when she was pregnant with me, she dreamt of stars, millions of stars that shown in the sky, and she grabbed one for herself and put it in her pocket. She loves stars, and it seems to be a sign for me in her heart. I have been thinking about this moment for a while now, it is beautiful and sad and lovely all at the same time.

So, P picked up the paper star and stuck it on the window and said, "When I look at the star I will think of grandma and uncle... I wish I had more to put on the window." I translated that for my Umma and she smiled and told him she loved him and gave him a kiss (which he did not wipe off his face). A beautiful quiet moment for the three of us. He does not want them to go, but assurances that we will see them again seemed to prevent him from crying. Five is such a lovely age.

I have a Korean mother-in-law whose relationship I have been trying to understand and appreciate for quite some time. Of all the "mothers" I have, I am struck by how much she has shown compassion, understanding, and love toward me these last three months. She has been very protective of me and has offered some really nice perspective and encouragement. She acknowledged how hard I have been working. That is huge! She reminded me of a couple of things that I really didn't notice. She has been somewhat bemused at the many misunderstandings I have had with Umma, but this time she was insistent that I listen in a different way than her usual "bull in a china cabinet" sort of way. She said that I need to tell my Umma how I feel, anger and all. "I have tried," I insisted, but she said, "Do it again. She needs to hear your heart." She said I have not really said how I FEEL, how I feel about her being in my life. I copped out and said that Umma never asked. She then said that my Umma needs forgiveness from me. I need to say it out loud, in English, Korean, whatever. No matter, it needs to be said for her but mostly for me. It occurred to me, I have told Umma to not worry about me, that I have a good life now, that I am OK and that she should return to Korea with peace in her heart and that there is nothing to forgive. But indeed I do need to forgive her because, you see, it was so clear that anger was prominently perched on my chest like an anvil. I do need to say "I forgive you." I have never said it.

I am finding it hard to say it in English or Korean. I asked my mother-in-law to say it for me, to translate it so that Umma can understand. But she said she would not do it—I need to do it. She is right. I have a task to do and I need to muster up the courage to do it. It is a whole lot harder than I thought. Forgive her.

I helped my Umma pack today, and my husband laughed and remarked that this has been the longest stretch of time and conversation I have had with her since she got here. I know! And what's more, I was a bit tearful about it too.

The evening of their departure...
I did it! I am free!!!

The three months are done and my Umma and brother are at JFK as I write this, waiting for departure in an hour and a half. It was not hard to say goodbye to my Umma, honestly it wasn't. We seem to have been getting along better as this time drew near, so I am at peace with how it all went down. I bought a Korean–English dictionary prior to their visit, and it has served me well if only to show my Umma the word "forgive." She said it out loud and it didn't seem to hit a spot, but I am glad I did it. Yes, it was for me too, and I felt a new kindling of warmth thawing my heart. I am beginning to heal. Still, I am not sure she was ready to be forgiven, or perhaps like her daughter, she didn't feel that this needed to be said? Still, I thought about it for a couple of days and realized that I need to do this for her so she can go with peace in her heart. I can process later as I know I have the capacity to truly forgive her. She commented on how hard this has been, and I didn't disagree as a polite Korean would have done. I just said, "Yes, it was, but I want you to go home with happy thoughts and peacefulness." And that was that. I might have copped out, but it's done, I meant what I said in my head, and someday I will mean it in my heart.

My brother on the other hand, I didn't want to let him go. He gave me the biggest hug, and I could not let him go. I am so grateful for him and so happy we got to spend time together.

So, my home feels suddenly huge! I felt like taking jetés around the room! I am the kind who unpacks the suitcases and puts everything away the first night back from vacation. The boxes of toys have been shifted around and the extra blankets and pillows stowed away, and I feel grand right now. It was all bittersweet as my children ran around saying, "Goodnight *wei haemi* (grandma) and *samcheon* (uncle)!" as they have for the last 90 days of their lives. It felt like always for them and so my big boy was a bit teary. My little stinker stayed true to his feelings. I asked him if he was sad that they were gone, and he looked me dead in the eyes and shook his head. Brutal but so true... I am guessing they will like Mommy a whole lot more now that she may be less crabby.

We are all exhausted but I will stay up to make sure the plane is up in the air... so I will be up till well past 1 a.m. this morning just to be sure.

It has been over a year since Umma and my brother left. I have found my peace with so much of their visit with much gratitude for my husband and friends, incredibly strong smart women. The time I had with my Umma doing ordinary things like shopping and laundry have remained with me—the sweet-

est apples need to be shorter than wider and three dryer sheets in the winter completely stops static cling. Those are the moments that have begun to solidify our relationship, and Umma is beginning to be my family.

"Becoming" Adopted

Kate Agathon

*At two years of age, I was adopted. At 31 years, I **became** Asian American. And at 32 years, I **became** a Thai adoptee.*

This is how I introduce my narrative to my friend Eddy, a Korean American actor in Los Angeles, who calls me on a Saturday afternoon. He is doing research for an upcoming role where he plays a character described as a twenty-something Korean adoptee raised in Wyoming. Knowing that I am a Thai adoptee who grew up in Colorado, he explains that I can offer him valuable insight into the adoption experience that only an adult Asian intercountry adoptee can provide.

I am flattered by his request and excited at the prospect of sharing my insights to make his character as realistic as possible. Specifically, I am eager to see an accurate representation of an adult Asian intercountry adoptee; one that avoids fish-out-of-water clichés and shows instead a multidimensional and complex individual whose identity is fluid and under constant negotiation. I emphasize to him that my "adoption story" does not begin on the day I was given up for adoption, nor on the day I was placed with my adoptive family. Instead, my "adoption story" begins when being both an Asian American and a Thai adoptee became a conscious state of mind that influences who I am and the values I hold. It is because of this intersection of my activism with the Asian American community and my recent discovery of memoirs written by adult Korean and Vietnamese adoptees that I am empowered to finally articulate my "adoption story."

The telling of "adoption stories" by adoptive parents and adoptees often chronicles the adoption process from the starting point of the adoptive family's decision to adopt a child and ends when the newly adopted child is placed with the adoptive family. This suggests that the adoption journey ends when the official paperwork is completed and a new family has been created. This is misleading, as many Asian intercountry adoptees (including myself) do not begin to construct their "adoption story" until they are adults and have had the opportunity to critically reflect on the experiences that have influenced their developing understanding of identity.

The sharing of "adoption stories" by adult Asian intercountry adoptees is of tremendous importance to facilitating a deeper understanding of our experiences. They enable us to identify, revisit, and uncover meaning in moments of psychological, cultural, and emotional difficulty through a critically reflective lens. Additionally, the emergence of narratives from adult Asian intercountry adoptees offers a unique and candid perspective into adoption storytelling. This is my narrative of how I spent the first 30 years of my life searching for my adoption identity, and how I discovered it through my political awakening as both an Asian American activist and a consumer of adoption knowledge produced by those who are themselves adult Asian intercountry adoptees.

What I consider the beginning of my true adoption journey occurred in graduate school, where I have become involved in Asian American advocacy and am writing a dissertation addressing adult Asian intercountry adoptee identity. I have begun to revisit my past, uncovering new meaning and taking note of past experiences, and my "adoption story" finally begins to emerge.

Becoming Asian American

Prior to college, I had grown up in a southeastern Colorado town nearly devoid of any Asians, save for our family and two Filipino families in town. During this time, my parents had made significant efforts to introduce me to my Thai heritage. They purchased cultural artifacts, took my brother and me to meet other adoptees at adoptee reunions, drove to Asian festivals in Denver, bought "Oriental Barbie" for me to play with, taught us to properly use chopsticks, celebrated Lunar New Year, and drove 100 miles to shop at the nearest Asian grocery store.

Despite their efforts, I did not feel any affinity to the country of my birth, nor did I feel any closer to my heritage. I simply wanted to assimilate into the general populace. In my hometown, you were either Latino or white. In the racial binary that I was faced with, I chose white, as I associated it with being financially better off (i.e., wearing name brand clothing and living in the "nice part" of town) and "All-American." I had learned what it meant to be "All-American" through John Hughes movies, *Seventeen* magazine, and the *Sweet Valley Twins* novels that I borrowed from my roommate at a summer enrichment program. I knew I could never emulate the blonde leads I saw in movies such as *Can't Buy Me Love* or *Beverly Hills, 90210*, a television show that I watched religiously. Instead, I settled for the imperfect Molly Ringwald and Winona Ryder. Not blonde, but full of angst attractive to an adolescent and unmistakably "American." In reflection, I think it is ironic that my family had painstakingly made the effort to incorporate Thai cultural artifacts or Asian-themed dolls and toys to influence my sense of identity, but I took my cue from popular culture that celebrated blondes, cheerleading, and whiteness.

I vividly remember an incident when I was a freshman in high school. Our class was participating in a diversity workshop that addressed racial stereotypes and perceptions. Predictably, the students taking the workshop with me viewed white people as successful and powerful. When the discussion turned to Asians, the students in the workshop described them as "weak" and "nerdy." I wanted to crawl under my desk. I said nothing to counter their assertions, especially when I felt equally uninformed. I equated "Asianness" with being foreign—not American. In that moment I felt confused. Even though my psychological allegiance was white, I felt inexplicably hurt and confused in ways I could not express. I felt cowardly for not speaking up and defending Asians, a group I could barely fathom myself. I did not recognize my Asian ethnicity until it was time to take the ACT college entrance exam, or apply for college scholarships for students of color. Even though I marked "Asian American" on my ACT, I truly considered myself as being white.

College afforded me a much larger exposure to Asian Americans who were not the "Fresh-off-the-Boat" immigrants or restaurateurs whom I had periodically encountered over the years, but students who were my age and who appeared to share similar interests. I seized the opportunity to get acquainted with my "Asianness." Unfortunately, my brief foray into learning about Asian Americans could only be described as a cultural tourism failure. Initially, I tried to socialize with them, but they were cliquish, refused to eat at non-Asian restaurants, and only hung out with each other. And most hurtful and puzzling of all, they did not seem to recognize Asian intercountry adoptees as "real" Asian Americans. Except for a handful of adoptees that "went Asian" by drinking boba teas, purchasing Hawaiian leis or Chinese ornaments to display from the rear view mirrors of their Japanese made cars, and removing their shoes at the entries of doorways—adoptees were largely criticized for acting "too white." To compound my confusion, I dated a Korean American whose mother thought I was acceptable because I was Asian American, but paradoxically unacceptable because I was not Korean American. Until then, I had not previously experienced this type of discrimination.

Ostracization notwithstanding, I took a few Asian American Studies courses, dated Asian American men, and was minimally involved with events held by the Asian Pacific American Student Services (APASS) advocacy office in an effort to try to gain a better understanding of what it means to be Asian American. Asian intercountry adoptees were nowhere to be seen in the Asian American Studies literature that I read, nor in the non-fiction books penned by Asian Americans that my parents purchased for me. This confirmed my suspicions that Asian intercountry adoptees were freaks that were neither Asian-American nor white and essentially belonged nowhere. It was not until years later when I was introduced to critical race theory in a graduate course that I realized I was looking at life through the lens of white privilege and racial covering.

I remember walking into my first graduate school class. My eyes scanned the room. In the sea of faces, I saw a lone Asian woman look back at me. Instead of sitting next to an Asian woman to show some kind of racial solidarity, I instead chose a seat next to a frizzy-haired blonde woman who was sporting an attractive Coach scarf and matching bag. Later that semester, that same Asian woman and I found ourselves paired up in a group research project. She expressed polite disappointment that despite my physical appearance, I was not at all Asian or interested in explaining to her the differences between Asians and Asian Americans. I told her I was adopted and did not divulge additional information. How could I tell her I could not bear to relive the bitter rejection that I had experienced by Asian Americans during my undergraduate years?

As a masters and later as a doctoral student in multicultural education, I was exposed to critical race theory. The most profound course I took in graduate school was one on multicultural education. It was a gateway course that I credit in helping me to analyze my past lived experiences. Only then did I begin to realize how politicized and problematic my identity was. It was then I began to recognize the glaring gaps in my life education. Why did I reject and accept my Asian-ness? Why was there always an unanswered question lurking in the background? Once I began to reevaluate my experiences through non-white eyes, I realized that no matter how I saw myself, what others saw was someone of Asian descent. I became more aware of who I was and what I knew, and challenged myself to contextualize my knowledge with my understanding of experience. I wrote my master's thesis on Asian American representation on prime time television, but it was only the first step into really uncovering who I am.

Later, I was given the opportunity to teach and design the curriculum for an Asian American Studies survey course. I was excited about the opportunity, but I was also extremely nervous. Despite having a Master's degree and a greater understanding of how to consider cultural backgrounds and unique experiences of individuals, I was not even sure if I *qualified* to be an Asian American. Plagued by my prior experiences, the question of whether or not I was *really* an Asian American haunted me. Was I being asked to teach the course on the assumption that my ethnicity made me an expert? I delved into as many books on the subject as I could. It was then I realized that being Asian American was not simply checking a box, but a conscious state of awareness. I began to see the correlation between my lived experiences and the systematic disempowerment of Asian Americans throughout U.S. history. I could no longer deny that I was unaffected by the social and political issues that are unique to Asian Americans. My transformation into an Asian American occurred when I became a critical practitioner of the world around me and I became more vigilant of my perceptions. My empowerment as an Asian American facilitated my deeper understanding of critically considering what it means to be adopted.

Becoming a Thai Adoptee

Throughout my life I have been exposed to various pieces of the adoption puzzle, but it was not until graduate school when I began to develop a critical consciousness that I started to put the pieces together. Prior to graduate school, the adoption literature that I had been exposed to was produced by adoptive parents, social workers, agency representatives, and other "experts" who specialized in Asian intercountry adoption. These articles in magazines and web sites promoting inter-country adoption served as the primary sources of my adoption knowledge and informed me of what my experiences were, predicted how I would turn out, and emphasized how "special" I was. Lacking the skills to critically deconstruct what I was reading, I accepted this knowledge as canon, and did not situate it the context of white privilege. Yet I knew something was wrong.

Despite reading these articles and even briefly working as an associate editor at an adoption magazine whose pages were filled with positive stories of love, religion, and culture keeping, I could not "locate" myself in the text. I found nothing that illuminated my experiences or feelings that I kept private. While playing the role of "happy, assimilated adoptee," I felt uncomfortable around adoptive families of Asian children with whom I regularly interacted with through the magazine. They wrote excitedly about purchasing en masse Chinese Empress

Barbies and about taking their Chinese adopted daughters to visit Mulan at Disney World. I knew from my own personal experiences that eating out at "authentic" Asian restaurants or shopping at Asian markets did not offer Asian intercountry adoptees an automatic membership into becoming truly Asian American. In fact, these culture-keeping efforts did not bring me any closer to Asianness or offer any life-changing insight. Instead, they just brought delayed confusion. There was a feeling of unease that I could not articulate when I corresponded with mothers who sent in photographs of their "adorable" adopted children in native dress. Later, I realized that feeling of unease was one of objectification.

Several years later, as a graduate student, I performed a pilot study of adoptive parents of Chinese children. During the study, I was invited to join a dozen families at a local Chinese restaurant to celebrate Lunar New Year. Our table was conspicuous not only because it consisted mainly of white parents with their Chinese children, but because they were the only table in the restaurant whose occupants were wearing "traditional" Chinese silk costumes. To my embarrassment, I noted the actual Asians in the room were not wearing "traditional" costumes. Under their contemptuous stares, I felt ashamed to be at that table and celebrating with well-meaning parents who were oblivious to my discomfort. I recall thinking these families were "playing Chinese" in the same manner my mother encouraged me to wear a Vietnamese *ao dai* to a performance of *Miss Saigon*.

Their overzealous efforts to maintain native culture was problematic because they approached culture keeping of Asian cultures through white eyes. This contributes to identity and cultural confusion later in life. For example, my family regularly attended musicals. As I grew up, I sang right along to scratchy tunes emanating from the vinyl records of *South Pacific* and *The King and I*, never realizing that they were fraught with a colonialist and marginalizing portrayal of Asians.

When *Miss Saigon* finally arrived in Denver in the early 1990s, my family was thrilled to see another musical portraying Asians. I can remember how emotional my mother got during the scene where video footage of real-life Vietnamese orphans was shown. I admit that I loved the musical. Over the next few years, I must have seen *Miss Saigon* six or seven more times. During some of these performances, part of me felt "special" to be the only Asian person in the audience. What I did not realize was that Asian Americans were not visible in the audience because they were actively boycotting it. And I did not learn the reasons behind the boycott until many years later.

While I was in the process of becoming Asian American, I came upon literature addressing the boycott where Asian American activists protested discriminatory hiring practices, the use of yellowface by lead actors, and the perpetuation of disempowering "Madame Butterfly" and "white savior" stereotypes. When I learned how *Miss Saigon* had galvanized the Asian American community into protest, I was both proud of being Asian American and horrified that I was unaware of how controversial a musical it was. I winced at the memory of Vietnamese adoptees and their families, whom I had met at a 1995 adoptee reunion, sharing my enthusiasm about the musical, because "their story" was being told. "Their" story may have been told, but from whose perspective? Who was producing this knowledge? As an Asian American activist, I now use *Miss Saigon* as an example of mainstream entertainment's continuous perpetuation of yellowface and use of harmful Asian stereotypes. Most importantly, I use it as recent example of organized protest by the Asian American community. I use the *Miss Saigon* episode in my life to illustrate how well-intentioned acts of culture keeping by white adoptive families can lead to conflicting identity issues later on.

Another example of culture keeping acts of love that can later lead to puzzlement or criticism from Asians or Asian Americans is the purchasing of ethnic Barbies. My own childhood was not immune from this. Starting in the early 1980s, my mother purchased for me in quick succession Oriental Barbie, Eskimo Barbie, and Spanish Barbie. I should mention these Barbies were not available in regular discount stores. They had to be special ordered (from an adoption magazine), and my parents took great pains to purchase these so I could have dark-haired Barbies that somewhat resembled me. During the late 1990s, the availability of Asian Barbies to mainstream toy stores and the introduction of Asian Princess-themed Barbies such as Chinese Empress Barbie, Princess of the Korean Court Barbie, Thai Barbie, Princess of Japan Barbie, and Sumatra Indonesian Barbie, made dark-haired Barbies more accessible than ever to adoptive families. What most adoptive families could not know is that from an Asian American perspective, this particular line of Barbies is problematic not only for their exotic appearance, but also for the marginalizing language on the text of the box encompassing the doll. One parent of a Cambodian adoptee purchased Thai Barbie for his daughter, claiming that it was the closest he would get to providing an "authentic" Barbie for his child and that she "would not know the difference." From the perspective of an Asian American, this is a cause for frustration, because non-Asians cannot seem to distinguish between different Asian ethnic groups. This contributes to the stereotype that all Asians are alike.

I became a Thai adoptee when I began to question the producers of the adoption knowledge that I had been exposed to throughout the majority of my life. I became a Thai adoptee when I felt confident enough to confront the lurking questions, the uncomfortable feelings, and confusion that I had from viewing life from another lens. This empowerment was facilitated by narratives written by (primarily Korean) adult Asian intercountry adoptees such as Jane Jeong Trenka, Jae Ran Kim, and Tobias Hubinette, who realized the urgency for an adoptee-produced critical knowledge base. By breaking away from traditional thinking, the development of an alternative perspective articulated in written and oral knowledge base made our previously unheard voices heard.

For me, my "adoption story" does not begin until three decades after I was officially adopted. It began when I became actively engaged in understanding what it means to be an Asian American, an adult Asian intercountry adoptee, and how Asian intercountry adoptees are precariously situated in the contexts of racialized kinship and ideological negotiations. I admit that I was hesitant to share my "adoption story" because it was something that was intensely personal; something that I wanted to keep for myself, not giving my parents full disclosure to something I held so close. But I realized that if I did not share this relevant knowledge, my experiences could not benefit other Asian intercountry adoptees and their adoptive families.

An emerging sense of core issues such as white privilege and racial identity construction enabled me to critically reflect upon my lived experiences and defining moments that contributed to my developing understanding of what it means to be both Asian American and also an Asian intercountry adoptee. These reflections transformed me from someone who was "Asian American" and "adopted" only in physical appearance or on paper, to someone who actively *became* both "Asian American" and "adopted." Together, my "Asian American" and "adopted" identities influence who I am and the values that I hold. Because I have a more comprehensive sense of what it means to be both Asian American and adopted, I now have the tools to truly share my "adoption story."

An Explanation of the Origin

Courtney Young

I have never let the imaginary lines that create a geographic grid of latitude and longitudes define who I am.

My genesis was at the coordinates of 36° 58' 0 N and 127° 57' 0 E—I couldn't have ended up further from the intersecting origin from where I came.

If you travel just over 10,500 kilometers east of my point of origin, you'll end up in the United States of America—my home. But, 36° 58' 0 N and 127° 57' 0 E are nowhere near the United States—those are the coordinates of Chungju City, South Korea.

I've never really thought about my adoption and the complexities of what it meant to be adopted until I was twenty-two. I graduated college and started working for Holt International, the agency my parents adopted me from. Up until that point I had never been around many Asian Americans, let alone other adoptees. Someone told me this job would be like baptism by fire. Whether she knew it or not, this was true—in more ways than one. People started asking me about my adoption experience before I even had the chance to think about it. I had no idea. I could not produce a legitimate response to the question without wondering about the answer as it came out of my mouth. After all, I didn't want people to think I'd never contemplated a monumental part of my life. Up to this point my thoughts and feelings had culminated due to a reaction to a question.

Although I vaguely remember my parents telling me; I always knew. The word *adoption* meant nothing to me. In fact, I resented the word in some ways, as if it labeled me, or gave causality to my very clear visible different looks in comparison to my brother. It would often go like this. "This is Jordan's sister." Perhaps a funny look from the observer, "She's adopted." I would always think to myself, "Wow, congratulations. You figured that out." It's like a small child learning that a cat is not a dog; however, there are of course, obvious distinctions.

At times even my closest of friends make comments. They say I am a bad driver because I am Asian. I am supposed to be good at math because I'm Asian. "He just likes you because you are exotic looking." "She can't drink much alcohol; she's Asian." But it gets old. I never blurted out in a group of people, "She just failed her math test because she's white." Sometimes I joke along with them for the sake of my sanity. I know what is coming; I better just say it first.

I don't dislike looking different than everyone else. In fact I enjoy it. I just do not like the apparent disregard some people have for a very obvious scenario. I am Korean, and my family, friends, and everyone else is Caucasian. If I ever wanted anything as an adoptee, it was to fit in without an explanation. The explanation always seems like a reason, as if I needed a reason to be a bad driver. No, I am simply a terrible driver. I believe my father having to read the driver's manual to me at the age of sixteen as I sat upside down on our couch eating popcorn is more indicative of why I'm a bad driver—not because I am Asian. I had failed the test four times prior.

A Different Kind of Resentment

My parents always told me that if I wished to try to locate my birthmother, they would support me. I was not interested. I was not interested in finding her. I was not interested in Korea, and I was not interested in being Korean. Perhaps I knew that going to Korea would mean the possibility of being vulnerable to the place I had come from, seeing myself in the children in the orphanages who are waiting for homes just as I was.

Going to Korea meant admitting that my life was not always perfect. I was not born into a family that had planned for me. It kind of worked out that way, but it doesn't change the fact that *I was not planned*. You see I have never been able to escape the reality of what an orphanage is. It is a place where children live because there is no one to take care of them; many will lie in their cribs for extended periods of time, no mom or dad to hold them. There is a reason pictures of babies in orphanages sharing cribs are so sad—because it is. If I went back to Korea, I would have to accept this, that I was never better than this, that I didn't have a mother and a father.

I never mulled over reasons my birth mother didn't want to keep me. So the resentment I felt was never towards her. I resented people asking me if I wanted to find her or if I thought about her. Maybe I was upset because I was being asked questions I had never asked myself. But why ask yourself questions when there is no reason to ask? I understand curiosity is human nature; if you ask anyone close to me, they will say it is most definitely in my nature. I feel the questions are out of sympathy, as if I lack a maternal bond with my mother, one that only my birth mother can fulfill; that my brother isn't my *real* brother. Those questions, the rhetorical ones with underlying cynical tones hurt me. It is again the need for an explanation. I had to explain that my relationship with my brother was just the same as anyone else's relationship with his or her sibling—probably better. The explanation of my origin is exhausting, not because I mind explaining my relationships, but because I have to defend the legitimacy of those relationships.

The question of blood has no validity to me. People have often asked me about the significance a relationship has when there is no blood-line between a family. That's a cheap and dirty way to be ignorant. The day someone can prove that a DNA-based relationship is more real than one that is not is the day I will rest my case. But that day will not come in my life time or the next—I can assure you of that.

Two Kinds of Love

I love my birth mother for loving me enough to keep me. That is something I will never forget. But I also know that when she chose to put me up for adoption, I was going to be someone else's daughter, and I love her even more for giving me my parents and my brother.

I was not an unwanted baby; my birth mother wanted me, but she knew she couldn't take care of me. She wanted me enough to give me to a family that could care for me. The love I have for my family transcends the barrier of blood, geographic location, and physical perception.

I am often asked if I feel selfish to have forgotten my roots, my culture, and Korea. I haven't forgotten anything. One cannot forget a place and a people he or she never knew. I am a Korean American. My ethnicity is Korean, but my culture is American. My roots are with my family, my friends, and the life I have lived for twenty-two years. My family has provided me with the kind of love that replaces any need or wants to search for a past I don't remember.

Do I ever wonder about my birth mother, or if she had any more children? Yes. I've always wondered what it would be like to look like someone, or for someone to say, "Is that you're daughter?" Not because he or she knows I'm adopted, but because you can tell. But of course I wonder these things. There is no doubt about the scope of adoption; children from all over the world traveling thousands of miles away from their origins to have a life they would not have had if they had stayed in their motherland. It is an amazing thing. I believe it is normal and natural to feel all sorts of things. But mine cannot be definitive for all adoptees. This is just my story.

I am starting to realize more about myself as an adoptee as I grow up. Although I claim not to be good at math, things make sense to me in equations. You could say X(Korea) + Y(Adoptive parents) got me to Z(My life now,) but we forget that X and Y have equations of their own and multiples steps to many equations made the sums of X and Y. So, Z is not just a product of X and Y; it is a product of many things combined.

My thoughts and feelings of Korea may change, but one thing is ever constant. I am blessed to have been adopted.

My name is Courtney Nicole Young and if you travel just over 10,500 kilometers east of my point of origin you'll end up in Eugene, Oregon—my home. My coordinates are 44.04°N and 123.1°W.

Homeland

Erin Elisabeth Ellis

Hazy memories of a distant past
fill my heart with a longing
It calls me to return someday
to a homeland far away
Thinking of the place where I was born,
all I can do is hope to meet them one day
So many have come from this land before me
to be given new lives, second chances, and liberty
I am here because I was given a chance to live
in a country to help me with my needs and disability
I thank the people who wanted to give me another chance
My life is better and I can live more independently
Even though everything happened for the best
I long to go back to the place where I am from
I hope to meet the people who gave life to me
Explore my roots and my ancestry
The call of the homeland is steady as a Janggu drum
Its steady echoes reach the depths of my heart
One day I will answer the call and return to the motherland
As a Gayageum picks up tempo and beat,
so my soul shall be that way when I return to my homeland

Like Mother Like Daughter

Rebecca Morris

Forty kilometers outside of Seoul, Kyung Hee plods along a muddy road. The wind whips through her thick, black hair slapping it up against her cheek. Drops of freezing rain intermittently hit her upper lip, providing moisture to her dry mouth. She does not know where she is going. The destination is irrelevant. She only knows this baby she carries in her arms is not her destiny. After a couple of hours, the young woman stops abruptly. She is tired and this place is as good as any. Her arms collapse, dropping the baby to the ground. A dead weight has been lifted. Wrapped in a tattered blanket, the baby is left shivering by the side of the road. Kyung Hee turns quickly and heads back toward her village. The child stares up in the sky watching the dark clouds roll in...

It's been estimated I was born in November, although it may have been as early as October. Whichever month it was, there is no documentation of the first few months of my life. It makes me sad and embarrassed that I do not know something so fundamental as one's place and date of birth. My birth date was arbitrarily written down on a blank space on a birth certificate. Since then I have continued filling in the blanks about the circumstances surrounding my conception and birth. My imagination has invoked an infinite number of theories ranging from the mundane to the absurd.

As a child, I grew up in a conservative Midwestern city in the United States. The local Chinese restaurant was the only exposure I had of Asian culture. Kimchee and rice were not the staples served at supper tables in my neighborhood. I ate red meat and potatoes. My friends had Swedish, Polish, German, and Italian surnames. My own family was of German and Dutch heritage. Ethnic diversity meant declaring oneself as a Catholic, Protestant, or Lutheran. Being born to a Korean woman had no significance in my life. I did not know her world, and she did not know mine. Besides genetic material, what did we share in common? Before long, that question would have its answer.

"I want a divorce," he said calmly. His eyes focused straight ahead unflinching. After two and a half years of marriage, my husband's words hit me in the face like projectile vomit. I was nauseous. How many times did he practice saying those words in the mirror before having the courage to say them out loud? I hadn't practiced hearing them. Over the last year, his manner had become increasingly secretive and aloof. Although we still maintained the façade of a happy couple, it should not have come as a complete surprise when the man whose name I still bear wanted to revert back to a life as a single, unencumbered man.

Does being abandoned as an adult have any less impact than being abandoned as a child? Perhaps the word abandoned is too strong in this context. Nonetheless, for the one being "left behind," it certainly feels the same. That sense of security is lost. My thoughts turned to my birth mother. She was the first person in my life who left me. What exactly happened?

A young woman stands outside a two-story building. A neon sign flashes above her as if advertising her vacant status. She takes a drag of a cigarette and inhales feeling a burning sensation in her lungs. Although it is February, she is scantily dressed. A chill is in the air and the night sky begins to pop with stars. She catches the eye of a young man and quickly flicks the cigarette onto the pavement squishing it with the toe of her high heel. The man nervously approaches the building. He fiddles with the zipper on his jacket. Without uttering a word, he signals with a glance and a jerk of the head. The young woman leads him into the building. Twenty minutes later she is outside lighting up another cigarette. She waits for the next man...

Perhaps it is spiteful of me to presume my birth mother was a prostitute. Honestly, how would I know this? Maybe she wasn't even a young woman. It is possible she was old enough to know right from wrong. Somehow viewing her as a struggling, impoverished, adolescent girl exonerates her. Until recently, I could not excuse her actions for any reason. It did not matter what her age was. Fact remains, she abandoned me. She left no note, no way of contacting her, nothing. Wouldn't a decent human being at least leave a letter explaining the situation? For all I know, she left me for dead. How could I forgive her?

The few months that followed after my separation from my husband put me in a whirlwind of anxiety and depression. There were days when I didn't know if I could function.

The only thing that gave me any solace was seeing my husband once a week. We chose to remain in contact. For both of us, it seemed to ease the sting of the separation by playing boyfriend and girlfriend. His mood drastically changed. He became more animated and alive like he was when we first dated. Being the part-time boyfriend with no strings attached was the ideal situation for him. For me, I was like a manic-depressive bouncing back and forth emotionally. In reality, it caused more damage. It only prolonged the inevitable. We needed to grieve so we could heal. We needed closure. That would soon come—but at a price.

From time to time, I wonder what my birth mother thought when she found out she was pregnant with me. Was there ever a time when she felt elated? Or did she always label me a burden? What did she think and feel? I can only speculate.

It is a typical Korean summer. The dead air is sweltering with humidity. Kyung Hee pulls her hair up off the nape of her neck. Feeling suffocated by the heat, she fans herself with one hand trying to cool her face. She looks down noticing her blouse. It is damp with perspiration and clings to the bulge peeking out from her abdomen. For a couple of weeks, she has tried to ignore it. But today, on this hot afternoon, she can no longer deny the truth. She tells herself it will only be a few more months. She feels afraid and alone. What has she done? Why is she being punished? She hates this baby...

What have I done? Why am I being punished? I asked those very questions when I learned I was pregnant. Had I not endured enough emotional turbulence in the past months? It was surreal. I was living a nightmare. It all came down to a tiny blue + in a tiny clear window of a pregnancy test. I was pregnant for the first time in my life at the age of 32... And I was separated from my husband.

Wanting confirmation of the pregnancy test, I made an appointment the next day at a clinic. There was no mistake. I knew the test was correct. I left the clinic with a positive result in one hand and a pamphlet in the other. Still in disbelief, I broke down laughing hysterically and crying at the same time. I remember the woman at the clinic congratulating me. I actually thanked her in return. Underneath it all, I just felt stupid.

The silence on the other end of the phone spoke louder than words when I spilled the news to my husband. He had lost the power of speech. "Uh huh," was his only response. He made no other attempt at voicing his opinion. I interjected and told him I wanted this baby. As a knee-jerk reaction, he said he would support my decision whatever it would be.

It suddenly occurred to me that I had a birth father. I always pictured one person involved. All that time, it was all about "her." She got pregnant. She gave me up. But there must have been a man involved in the equation. Who the hell was he?! After all, I doubt I was a product of Immaculate Conception. Yet, all my anger had been directed at a woman. She was to blame. But what about him?

Here I was pregnant, just like her. The father of my baby was relinquishing any responsibility. He wanted the decision to be mine alone. Did she experience the same thing? Did my birth father not want to take any responsibility either? For the first time in my life, I could empathize with this woman. I could sympathize as well. She was someone like me.

After a lot of agonizing soul searching, I could not in good conscience bring a baby into this world. My relationship with my husband was tenuous at best. There was no stability. My own parents divorced when I was 7 years old. I knew I did not want my child to be shuffled back and forth between two homes. In reality, that was the path our relationship was following.

What recourse did my birth mother have when she found out she was pregnant? It was the late 1960s, and she was living in a poor country. Did any medical intervention exist for her? If so, did she ever weigh that option? It was difficult to comprehend why she had me. In the end, she got rid of me. There were many times growing up I sat alone and cried. I wished she had gotten an abortion. I didn't understand how she could have left me. I was feeling alone with no one to turn to. Even though my adoptive family loved me dearly, I did not feel a connection to them. I felt extremely isolated.

The idea of giving up my baby for adoption never crossed my mind. Such a selfless act was not in my character. How did she find the strength to do it? I was beginning to admire this woman. Maybe I didn't give her enough credit. It would have tortured me to give up my child. Luckily, a choice was available to me. It was a choice I would not regret. But one for which I would seek absolution.

The morning of the procedure I felt numb. I arrived at the clinic and waited for my name to be announced. As I stepped inside the hallway, I found myself in an assembly line. I saw the faces of other women all in various stages of this finely choreographed production. Each woman had her own reason for being here. But we all endured the same outcome.

The entire process took about three hours. Afterwards, my husband drove me to my apartment complaining the whole way. The drive home was tense and filled with emotion. His method of coping with the situation involved ranting about my lack of common sense and assigning blame. His own hurt and pain would not permit him to console me. Outside, I was fuming with anger. Inside I was dying.

Was my action forgivable? I have to believe that my decision was right for me at the time. I know my birth mother did what was right for her. She can be forgiven. Often it seems like the most reprehensible act cannot be justified. But life is not black and white. There are predicaments that have no simple resolve. Sometimes the solutions are based on survival.

When I was a little girl, I fantasized that my birth mother would find me. I pretended she came from a prominent, affluent family and wanted to lavish me with affection and material possessions to make up for abandoning me. Maybe all adoptees have that fantasy in some fashion. But she never did come to my doorstep. I still have to play out that scenario in my mind.

Fifty-three years have past since my birth. Any notions of finding my birth mother have been buried for over twenty years. Finally, I have resolved to my satisfaction any issues related to this woman. She no longer torments me. Yet, it is on an autumn day that she makes her first contact. Lying in the mailbox is an envelope with a stamp from a foreign country. The letter is thrown on the kitchen table with the assumption it was delivered to the wrong address. The name on the envelope reads Park S.M. but it is written so haphazardly it is barely legibly. Two days pass and the letter still sits on the table. I grab it to write the words "return to sender." I suddenly notice the name Park. It was the surname given to me at the orphanage. This letter is for me. I can feel my heart pounding in my chest. I have secretly waited for this moment all my life. I rip open the envelope to discover two pages of a handwritten note. I cannot read a single word. It's written in Korean...

"Korean War Baby—Devil Child"
My Journey of Self-Identity

Don Gordon Bell

A young Korean mother cautiously brings her four-year-old son and one-year-old daughter through the streets of downtown Seoul. The young woman knows that because her children's father was a "foreign devil," that they will always be cursed and rejected by her people. She dyed their light brown hair with black shoe polish to hide them better, but their faces still look strange and noticeable. (Korean people call her children "*TuiGi/튀기* " a slang word that meant "evil spirit" or "child of the devil."

The young mother hears a rumor; she should find the flag of her children's father flying over a building near the city hall. Unwanted children were being collected and sent to homes in their fathers' countries. The determined young mother finally finds the flag of their American father waving over the Reception Center of World Vision. A kind-looking foreigner, a man in his fifties, notices them lingering near the gate. The man, Harry Holt, approaches them with a warm smile. Looking into his strange round eyes, her fear diminishes. There she sees a deep concern and love. He gently reached out his strong hands, took her son's hand and wordlessly he guides them through the gates.

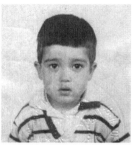

Jun Yong Soo / 전용수 / (Donald Gordon Bell)
Korean passport photo

"What ARE you?" My Search for Identity

My name is Donald Gordon Bell, I was that young boy and my younger sister, Lorelei Susan Bell, was the baby. We were some of the earliest Holt adoptees. My flight was the first group from Holt, and my sister was on the first chartered flight in 1956. I believed that our mother gave us up, in love but with much sorrow, hoping for a good American family to take us and provide what she could never give us under the circumstances. I cannot imagine what she thought or felt. Did she leave us and just forget? I don't believe so, and by reading and hearing how many birth mothers suffered through the years wondering what happened, it has helped me mentally understand and forgive.

Throughout my life I have tried to deal with "Who AM I?" In my mind as a five year old, deep in my spirit, my *"Inner Child"* was pierced and wounded. My self-identity was always linked to *"My Adoption Story"* that I would recite without emotion to curious folks who looked at my white parents then asked, *"This is your son?"*

Children of War

I was born January 25, 1952, eighteen months after the start of the war. My sister was born June 9, 1955. A woman with *two mixed-race children* would have had an almost impossible task to take care of us. I never felt angry towards my birth mother because my adoptive parents, both Christian, raised us to understand my birth mother's predicament. I was told that we are adopted into God's family. Only in my mid-thirties did I begin to comprehend these Christian teachings personally.

My Korean name Yong Soo 용수/容秀 means "Face Excellent." The word "adopt" comes from Latin, "ad" meaning "add to or take" and "optare" means "by Choice." So adopt means to "take by choice" a child. Roman Laws of Adoption implied that the 'past identity' was completely gone. The 'new identity' through adoption was recognized as equal to a biological child. My identity encompasses both my genetic and adoptive heritage.

City of Angels—Los Angeles, California

My adoptive parents managed a downtown apartment building in L.A where we lived my first year in America. Shortly after my arrival, my adoptive mother got sick and was hospitalized. I spent several months with her younger sister, Katie, and her family. I bonded with her as a second mother. They lived in a huge house with yards and dogs. Then suddenly, I went back to the downtown apartment and had a hard time adjusting back to first mother.

To The Valley

After my sister arrived, we moved to the San Gabriel Valley. We were surrounded by strawberry fields and orange and apple groves. We were middle-class suburban America, and my Korean sister and I matched each other like a pair of shoes. My school was mainly Caucasian but a few Mexican kids from migrant families attended. At first they spoke Spanish to me and insisted that I had some Mexican blood. I had a few problems with some bullies at two elementary schools I attended, but I was quick to fight back so they left the crazy '*Jap*' or '*Chink*' alone. No one seemed to know about Korea or the '*forgotten war.*' In every grade on the first day of class, I dreaded the teacher introducing me as the Adopted Orphan from Korea. I spent years having extra home schooling from my mother and loved to go to the city library and look at picture books until I could read. Researching in the library improved my reading so that by grade six I was reading senior high school level material.

Until junior high school I had frequent episodes of sleep walking; my parents would find me outside and have to wake me up. Sometimes I had nightmares and shouted in Korean until someone woke me. I scared my fellow boy scouts on a few camping trips. "*Don't mess with the Oriental guy, he's nuts.*" I don't remember what I was dreaming, but in university I had some hypnosis with a psychiatrist that brought up some vivid memories, most were like flashes of dark and noisy scenes, not of war but scary things. A child's view of life I suppose.

"Are You Half-Asian?"

All my life people would ask me, *"What ARE you? Asian or something?"* My identity was unclear. Which *'box'* did I check? Many Asians would ask me what my Asian *'ethnic background'* was. Not fully Asian. I was half-Korean... half-*something*. I felt divided, a split-personality. I trained in Asian martial arts for about eighteen years. I earned Black Belts in TaeKwonDo, Kenpo Karate Iaido (using real Katana samurai swords). I studied Escrima, Filipino Bolo/knife, and stick fighting; I won a number of trophies at tournaments throughout the southwestern United States. I found a way to 'discover' my Asian-ness in the fighting arts.

High School Days

Junior high was nothing special for me. Our school was very mixed racially with Asians, Mexicans, and lower middle class Caucasians. In high school they started a busing program, and half of my eighth grade class was bused fifteen miles away to South Hills High School. That school had students from upper middle class families. We were a very odd and divided student body. Dating was only within your economic group, and we in the *lower* class were called the *Northerners* since were came from north side of the San Gabriel Freeway. My circle of friends came from both sides, but I dated only the *Northern girls*.

Curiously a Japanese/American girl was forced by her father to break up with me. Her Japanese mother was a *military bride* and seemed to like me, knowing I was half Korean. Her father was another story since he suffered in prisoner of war camps with brutal Korean guards. I didn't know the details of Korea being under the Japanese Empire at that time. After Vietnam I understood how he felt.

Off to War—Like Father, like Son

The Vietnam War was escalating and activists were marching against the war. Like my birth father, I volunteered to serve in a far off land, trying to help people I knew nothing about to remain free. I served with an elite Long Range Reconnaissance unit of the U.S. Marines in Vietnam, volunteering to be with the *elite of the elite*, 1st Recon Battalion, Recon Lurps, a Recon Marine. I experienced many of the horrors of war, fought and killed, to survive.

From my teens until age thirty-three, I learned to drink, fight, cuss, and live wildly with total abandonment. I reveled in hard living and playing. How did I survive? Only by the grace of God. I have stayed free from drug addiction only because I fear God. I threw myself into riotous living like the Prodigal Son, and like my biblical counterpart, I had broken off contact with my adoptive parents.

Years later in 1985 I went through a series of events that led me to finally believing and trusting in Jesus Christ. I truly became a Christian and went through long periods of repentance, felt deep remorse for all my '*liaisons without names or faces.*'

"They're Going to Put Me in a Movie"

After leaving the Marines, I went to college without direction or purpose. Then by fate I took a trip to the Philippines in 1975. The Vietnam War movie *Apocalypse Now* was in pre-production and casting extras. The local casting director noticed my USMC tattoo, and introduced me to Director Francis Coppola. When he heard I had been a Marine Recon, in-country Vietnam, and fired weapons in combat, I was hired as a military advisor. I trained extras on weapons, infantry tactics, and exiting helicopters; and made sure they wore uniforms and equipment correctly, helping them to look and act like real troops at war.

A Tale of Two Women

While filming I met Quan, a Vietnamese/Cambodian/French beauty. After filming ended, Quan moved in with me. I was thinking about proposing to her but she had family waiting in France. While I was '*on location*,' on a new war film, she finally got through by phone to tell me that she had suddenly received her visa to France and must leave right away. I rushed back to Manila, but she had left that morning. Quan's letter weeks later told me she was pregnant with my child. I wrote her that I would move to France, but in her next letter to me, Quan had a job, had met a French businessman fluent in Vietnamese and they had married. The last letter I received contained a photo of a baby; asking permission for *monsieur* to adopt my son! I wrote back "*Oui, but of course*," with mixed feelings of relief and guilt. I have lost contact with my Vietnamese son, but Quan promised he would grow up knowing my name. My hope is that one day he will search for me.

Before Quan, I dated Susan, a Filipina actress. Another man proposed to her and later I saw her as she was preparing a fiancée visa for America. She was obviously pregnant and I asked her if I was the father. She said "No." Six months later, I was shocked, when I received a letter with a picture of '*my daughter*' with the explanation that Susan had lied to me because she felt she had a better deal with the man she married. "Your daughter will know your name," she promised.

"You Must Be My Bio-Dad"

In 1985 at a coffee shop in Manila, I heard someone call my name. "Don Bell! Is that you?" There was Susan, and beside her a nine-year-old girl. MY daughter looked curiously at her mother. She said with a sweet smile, "You must be my Bio-Dad!" I met her adoptive father and younger half-brother and spent several days with them. I have been fortunate to maintain contact with my daughter, who is now married, making me the biological granddad of two.

Return to the Motherland

Since 1995 I have lived and worked in South Korea, teaching English. In 2005 I married a Korean woman, who is a police officer. I understand the Korean people's mindset on the issues of adoption quite well, always discussing with my students the multiple issues involved. Students are usually curious why I don't look "American." Some are surprised, shocked, disappointed when they learn that I am one of Korea's *first exports.* Attitudes are *slowly* changing but the majority of Koreans would never adopt a child, even if it is "whole" and not "damaged." I cannot get angry; that is just the way most believe. Living here has given me more understanding, but my mindset is still Western and clashes with the Asian ways every day.

I understand the feelings of loss that "full blooded" Korean adoptees also have experienced in losing their heritage by being sent away from our Motherland. We all suffered, whether we were adopted as a baby or older child. We must consider though this inconvenient truth: that all of our mothers faced an almost impossible task of keeping and raising us due to lack of resources from family and little government aid. We, who have been raised in Western societies, can only try to understand how the Korean people think concerning adoption. I was one of the twelve charter members of GOA'L when founder Ami Nafzger met in 1997 to discuss a group to help adoptees returning get help in their search, finding a job, apartment, etc.

Not a Devil Child anymore, but an Adopted son of GOD!

I am Scottish, English, Korean, Apache, Mexican, Spanish… and through God's adoption, a son of GOD. Under God's law we are '*adopted children*,' with full legal rights. What a Heavenly Adoption Plan! Adoption by GOD. His forgiveness, mercy, and love are unconditional. Like adoption on earth though it is still a process that we must work through. It is a life long journey.

In the Hands of God

Sara Campion

"The Nations will see your righteousness and all kings your glory; you will be called a new name that the mouth of the Lord will bestow. You will be a crown of splendor in the Lord's Hand, a royal diadem in the hand of your God."
Isaiah 62:2-3 (NIV)

Love. The greatest desire of the human heart. As I begin to fully comprehend the details of my adoption, I have learned much about love and the power it has to change lives for the better. I have found healing in my story, and more importantly, purpose.

I was born in Seoul, South Korea, in 1979, but this story begins with my mom, Nancy. One Friday night in 1966 my mom, who was 16 or 17 at the time, watched the 1958 film *The Inn of the Sixth Happiness*. It is the true story of missionary Gladys Aylward portrayed by Ingrid Bergman. Aylward believed her purpose was to go to China. While in China Aylward rescued 100 orphans during the Japanese invasion by guiding them over mountains on foot to safety. It was while watching this scene in the movie from her living room floor that mom decided she, as she puts it, "wanted one of those children."

December 1970 my father arrived home from Vietnam and met my mother. In May 1973 they married and moved to North Arlington, New Jersey. A few months later mom had a very special dream. The following are her words:

"In the Autumn of 1973, one harvest moon night, I was looking out of my bedroom window and I said: 'Please God, let me have a baby.' That night, a Friday, I had a prophetic encounter which might I say I knew nothing about. I dreamed I was in an Asian country in a small pond giving a baby girl a bath and all around me was a beautiful feeling of love, which I know now, was the love of God. And in the dream I kept saying 'I didn't give birth, but this is my baby girl who I am holding.' The baby had her arms around my neck. I could feel this and I was floating in this incredible feeling of love. I had never felt this kind of love in my life. It was a Godly love. It was waves and waves of this beautiful love. I felt so secure and peaceful. I was floating in it. I remember going around in circles holding her, like when you see a person spinning around and around in a movie and I kept saying, 'This is my baby, I didn't give birth to her, but this is my baby.' There were other Asian people bathing their babies, and I could feel this bubble of love around us. I fought waking up because I could feel this love around me."

International adoption was not as common in the 1970s, so it did not occur to my parents to adopt then. In 1974 my parents moved and befriended a neighbor named Lillian. One day mom broke down crying about not being able to have a baby. Lillian told mom she would ask her son if he knew people in his church that could help. The next day Lillian gave mom the phone number of the mother of a nineteen-year-old Korean girl in her son's Bible study. Her mother had adopted several children and was well associated with an adoption agency. Mom phoned to get more information, and my parents began the process of adoption from Korea. Soon after, the doors to adopt from Korea were closed due to some issues that had to be resolved. My parents decided to wait.

In 1979 my parents relocated to a small town in upstate New York. That summer they contacted a social services agency about adopting and were informed the problems with adoption from Korea had been resolved and adoption was re-opened. December 1979 they received a referral and their first picture of an infant girl—me. I had been abandoned and given the name Choi, Mee-Na. I was premature, malnourished, and burned. They estimated my birth date to be early July 1979. The story of my arrival in my mom's words:

April 19, 1980

Kennedy Airport. Seven children arriving from Korea. Parents from N.Y, Boston, Pennsylvania, and Maine all anxiously waiting. The first baby that is off the plane is mine. A 17 hour trip and Sara arrives with an upper respiratory infection. She is very, very tired. She cried for 17 hours and the stewardess can't wait to hand her to me. Sara is very red in the face from crying and they hand her to me. She put her arms around my neck, collapsed, and fell asleep. Her arms could not be pried away. Rich, Sara's father, tried and couldn't do it. It was the fulfillment of what God showed me in my dream seven years later.

When I arrived to my parents I was 9 months old and weighed sixteen pounds. My attachment to my mom especially was immediate. I am told I kept my arms wrapped around her neck for months after my arrival. It never mattered that I was dripping in sweat or uncomfortable. Mom had to be in my line of vision at all times, and if she left the room I would cry my eyes out. It seems as though I have always known the story of mom's dream. My parents were always very clear about their desire to adopt me, so I never felt sorry for myself or saw my adoption as an act of pity or a last resort. It was and is an honor to be adopted.

Within any abandoned child there are seeds of rejection and fear, even in an infant. Those seeds in me were watered and fed by certain peers growing up. I had many good friends that I still love dearly, but a small handful of people said terrible things to me. In my area of New York, I was the only Asian girl for miles. The continuous negative remarks taught me to defend myself by building up walls, to reject before being rejected, to hide and go numb emotionally so that after awhile I never actually realized I was in pain. Deep down I believed everything said about my so-called flat face, slanted eyes, and that I would never have a boyfriend or husband because of my ethnicity. Just like any well-planted lie, these comments played over and over in the back of my mind so much so that they started to sound like the truth and felt very natural.

I do not remember ever telling my parents what was said to me. They would have been livid. Maybe that is why I did not tell them. Why a racist remark would ever feel truthful or natural is beyond me now, but to a child or adolescent surrounded by a reality that reinforced the "truth" of those remarks was easy to believe. Eventually, the comments subsided, but I did not need to hear them anymore because I allowed them to become a part of me. I allowed them to define who I was.

On Memorial Day weekend 1992 we were in church, and during worship a friend passed a small piece of paper to my mom. The friend's name was Jane Lawson, who was loved by many. She was known for her wisdom and her talent for writing poetry. On the paper was the following:

> *"You shall be like a blue stone in a King's crown,*
> *full of beauty and pleasing to God."*
> *For Sara 5/24/92*

I can still see Jane handing the slip of paper to my mom and my mom showing it to me. Although I did not understand it then, she kept it safe for me and I have it today.

This verse was how God saw me. Pleasing to Him. It was also a glimpse of what was going to happen in my life to transform me into this "blue stone." Precious gems, like diamonds, undergo immense amounts of heat beneath the Earth's surface to become the valuable diamonds treasured by many. The most precious gemstones are refined by fire and proven to be authentic. The excess is cut away to reveal a perfect stone. Sounds like life to me!

Fall of my senior year my dad moved out of the house. Less than two months later mom's closest friend died of cancer at age 36. By this time my American brother, who was adopted as an infant when I was 3, was at his worst. After years of doctors, evaluations, hospitalizations, medications, and wrestling with the school system to get him into a special program, my brother was diagnosed with a developmental disorder. One of the many effects of his disorder was a lack of control over his emotions, which led to violence. A couple from church who knew how to handle kids like my brother agreed to take him in. It was the best place for my brother and I am thankful. With all of the problems in my family, I would not trade them for a lifetime of pain-free living. They are my family, no matter what.

In college I earned a Bachelor of Arts degree in music. Music helped me build self esteem, improved my grades, and provided a sense of safety. I could bury my nose in a piece of music and forget everything else. It was after college that everything I had been through caught up with me: a broken home, racist insults, overwhelming fear, and a heart full of un-forgiveness and confusion left me empty and depressed. It seemed as though I was invisible on the outside with a bottomless black hole on the inside. I fluctuated between either numbness or feeling so much pain it took my breath away. It was at this point that I started digging through my faith in Christ for the healing I knew I needed. Good friends, church, prayer, worship music, books, Bible study, and staring at the ceiling thinking for hours were all a part in my healing. I slowly felt wholeness fill me and release me from the pain.

In 2008 I shared the phrase Jane wrote for me with friends from my church. They immediately thought of the blue Hope Diamond, known as "the blue diamond of the crown." I learned that blue diamonds are very beautiful, rare, most desired, and valuable. When those words filled the atmosphere of the room, I felt my "worthlessness" tighten itself around my waist not wanting to let go.

I am just beginning to accept this as a journey that has no end, but that is fine with me. I like knowing that there is always more goodness to be found.

In a world where we amass as much wealth as possible and engage in temporal pleasures to numb our pain, I dare you to be different, I dare you to love.

"Yet God has made everything beautiful for its own time. He has planted eternity in the human heart, but even so, people cannot see the whole scope of God's work from beginning to end."
Ecclesiastes 3:11 (NLT)

Biological Mother

Jo Rankin

you tried your best
to cut the cord—
destroyed a nest
beyond afford.
my fate was filed
and soon defined:
a lonely child
you left behind.
since you and i
may never be
together in
reality,
should i go on
and try to solve
the questions which
have since evolved,
or should i quit
while i'm ahead,
and try to do
without, instead?
such simple words
for mother's pearl.
from me, with love,
your inchon girl.

.

Mommy

Jo Rankin

you tried your best
to fill our void,
then built a nest
we both enjoyed.
my fate improved --
was redefined
when inchon soil,
i left behind.
since you and i
will always be
together for
eternity,
i finally tried
to reach resolve
with questions which
have since dissolved.
now i can move
and look ahead,
and share my life
with you, instead.
such simple words
for mommy's heart.
from me, with love,
your counterpart.

The Ultimate Sacrifice:
A Fairytale Adoption Story

Michael Marchese

I was born in 1971 in Vietnam. Four years later Vietnam fell to the Communists. My mother knew they would not tolerate Amerasian people. She feared her children would be in danger under the new government, so to keep us safe and to give us the best possible chance to live a happy life, she made one of the greatest sacrifices a mother could make: she put my sister and me up for adoption. One day in 1975, my mother brought Tina (my sister) and me to the Holt Adoption Agency. Leaving the two of us in a room full of children, my mother simply walked away.

At that time in Vietnam, people were stealing children from their mothers and selling them on the black market for profit. Tina, being older, remembered that my mother always taught us never to leave her side, so she followed my mother and left me in the room by myself. Her last image of me is watching me playing with a truck on the floor by myself.

My mother and my sister went home together, but came back the next day to find me. I was already gone. From what they understood, the plane to America that I was supposed to be on crashed, killing everyone on board. For twenty-four years they thought I was dead, not knowing that I had been put on another plane. I landed safely in America and was adopted by a wonderful family, the Marcheses.

Tina came to America three months after me to a family from Baltimore, Maryland. She spent her first few years in America in Baltimore and then moved with her foster family to Lakewood, California. At fifteen, she married a Vietnamese man named John. They now have three kids: John, Alexandria, and Ashley.

My sister was reading a magazine about the 25th anniversary of the fall of Vietnam in 2000. In the magazine, there was an article on Holt Adoption Agency. Tina brought the magazine home and asked her daughter Alexandria to go on the Internet to find Holt's telephone number. With encouragement from her husband and family, Tina finally made the call to Holt to see if there was any information on me. Four months later, she received a call saying that they found a match, and she proceeded with the process to find me.

In December 2000 I received a call from Holt. Thinking it was going to be a charity call, I never expected them to tell me my sister was looking for me. After Holt contacted me, they contacted my sister, who then called my mother, whom she had been in contact with since 1996. My mother still thought I had died in the plane crash. I can't imagine how she felt when Tina told her she found me. Once all the paperwork was cleared, I got Tina's telephone number and gave her a call. We talked for five hours! We were both in total shock and many tears were shared. It was great to know that she was alive and that I could talk to her.

It was 2001 when I booked a ticket to Los Angeles to see Tina for the first time. I took off from the Newark, New Jersey, airport with my cousin, Jen, and my best friend, Dave. I was very nervous. During the five hour flight, so many thoughts ran through my head. What does my sister look like? Will she like me? Will I be able to recognize her after all this time?

I really had no reason to be nervous. I was amazed as I entered the airport terminal. There were at least 100 people waiting to see me. Balloons, flowers, and a local television station greeted me with thundering applause. In the middle of all the festivities stood my sister. All four feet, ten inches of her. It was not hard to recognize her as she was a spitting image of me. She was crying and hugged me for at least ten minutes. We went back to Tina's house for a well-deserved and fantastic party with more than 100 family members and friends. Our story was on the 11 p.m. local news that night. We spent the weekend catching up on being brother and sister. A couple of months later Tina came to Philadelphia to meet my adoptive parents. My parents welcomed Tina as one of their own daughters.

❖

In 2006, my dream of meeting my birth mother was finally coming true. Tina, Ashley (my niece), Jonelle (my wife), Joe and Marty Marchese (my parents), and I went to Vietnam to see my mother for the first time since she left me at the orphanage. As we passed through customs and out the airport doors, I saw a group of people waiting to welcome people off the plane. I saw a tiny woman burst through the crowd and run to me as fast as she could. She held onto me and repeatedly said, "I love you. I miss you. Are you okay?" It was amazing to see my mother for the first time. I told her I loved her and thanked her for making such a sacrifice. Another surprise awaited me in the airport: my half-sister, Mei Lyn, whom I had never met or spoken with before.

I do not resent my birth mother for what she did. I have had a wonderful life without regrets, and I am grateful for everything I have and for my ever-growing family. I only wish that all adoption stories could be as successful and rewarding as mine. As for my birth father, someday I hope to have the same joyous reunion as well.

Arriving

Jenny Foster

My life has been a journey of self discovery, although whose hasn't? I was adopted at 6 months, spent my early childhood in the rural country of southern Indiana, and then migrated to Michigan with my single mom and homemade brother, casualties of a divorce from when I was 3. Our family was quite unconventional—given the time frame of the mid '70s and '80s, and one that had had more than its share of loss.

My mother remarried when I was in sixth grade to a brute of a man who left countless injuries and imprints on our consciousness—but whom I've come to see with gentler eyes in adulthood, especially since he passed away suddenly during my sophomore year in college. Meanwhile, my adopted father remained in what is now considered a civil union with a man who I embraced, respected, and loved as a second— or is it third? fourth?—father. I would often count the days to when I could see them—they let me drink coffee! With plenty of milk and sugar of course—spending lazy summer visits at their house, road-tripping to the country in Kentucky to visit my grandmother and uncle, or sharing winter holidays, snuggled up next to the couch with their miniature schnauzer, Benji, watching the fall of snowflakes outside their living room window. They also died, my adopted father when I was

16, and his partner when I was 20, both from AIDS-related complications.

Through all of this, I felt badly for my mother—having left the house upon high school graduation with a fervent vow never to return, that can only be made with teenage intensity because I couldn't bear the glance or judgment of our stepfather, but loving her nonetheless. I distinctly remember hurrying home again once he passed away. My mother needed help getting outpatient surgery, which was successful, and from that point forward our relationship was easier as well as between her and my brother, who'd left many years prior under similar circumstances.

We were blessed when she remarried for the third time to a kind, strong, wonderful man, who would later adopt me as an adult, our family seemingly complete once again. By this time I had my first child, a daughter, and she had a bona fide grandfather. I explained to my husband that all through my life there seemed to be countless losses, but with this adoption, I was finally claiming family instead of losing it.

My first daughter, still a baby, peeked at us out of her stroller when we sat down to celebrate after the courthouse. We had reservations for dinner at a restaurant in Hawaii Kai with a picture-window view of the sun descending over the ocean, lighting up the water in brilliant blues and golds. I still remember the waiter asking us if we were celebrating a special occasion. We all looked at each other and laughed, not sure how to answer. My mother finally said we were celebrating a "family reunification." The waiter smiled and nodded beneficently—afterwards we were presented with a custom dessert, the plate decorated with "Happy Reunification Day" spelled out in chocolate syrupy letters. We laughed again, wondering what the kitchen had thought of this—that crazy looking *haole* and Asian family part of an odd religious cult?

Sadly, this father too would succumb to cancer when my daughter was not quite two. I sat by his side daily, something I hadn't been able to do with any of my other fathers, holding his hand, knitting or changing the CDs to his favorite singer as he slept through the day and night until he was at peace at last. I still wonder if he heard us, if my daughter's footsteps pitter-pattered in his ears, if he felt the love that was surrounding him before he left us forever.

Because she was born in Hawaii, my daughter had never seen snow, delighting in stomping on the porch with her boots wondering at the white powder that magically fell from the sky. In her youthful exuberance she did not understand why grandma was sad or why grandpa was sleeping and chirruped her toddler demands and needs through the days, making us smile despite our hearts were breaking again. Soon after he passed, the rains came, pelting the roof, the windows, the walls with icy rain drops that matched my heartbeat.

Long before my eldest daughter was born, I came home to visit, taking a hiatus from graduate school, having a psychological crisis about what I was doing with my life and where I was going. I had just finished teaching ESL in Korea and loved every minute of it, embracing the consciousness that I was the "other" in both Korea and America, and finally accepting that it was just who I was. That belonging was an internal matter of the heart that was self created with chosen family and friends that I had to stop looking for "home" and "family" outside of myself and embrace those seemingly holy words within. And while this concept sounds reasonable, I still struggle with it, even though I've built a home in the foothills of the Koolau Mountains with two children's voices echoing within our walls.

I had managed to travel the world, unveil the mist of my birthplace, and share laughter and learning with children who looked just like me when I was younger. I'd backpacked and camped along the three shores of the southern peninsula, caught the *Tong-il* train and sat with my legs dangling out the back door watching the green verdant countryside fade into the concrete fingers of Seoul—making lifelong friends that I keep to this day. After my contract ended in Korea, I'd camped along the eastern coast of Australia and, after a short stint back on the U.S. mainland, lucked out on a scholarship to the University of Hawaii studying writing and in my free time learned to catch waves on the south shore of Oahu. What was wrong with me, then, why wasn't I happy? Why was I still struggling with the thought of home or family? And my yet-to-be-adopted father answered with calm simplicity: *hills and valleys, Jenny, hills and valleys. Sometimes you're in the shade, and the next moment you're in the sun, but it always changes.*

Right. It was so easy and so clear. And later I'd learn the same tenets in t'ai chi, from my rosy-cheeked beer bellied teacher. Letting go. Acceptance. Stay in the moment. I randomly wonder if my last father knew about t'ai chi, realizing I don't know too much about when or how he grew up or what his life was like before he came to us. And despite the simple truth, his words didn't calm me for long, the tempest inside my heart surged forward again but I waited for it to recede. It wouldn't last forever, he was right. And life moved on. I returned to Hawaii, graduating while working full-time, married; stepping up in the world, paying taxes, an average productive member of society.

Often you hear people say: everything changes when you have children. That a-ha moment happened to me both times, though slowly, not quite the lightning strike I've heard others experience. Since what was before a thought, or a pure act of will—that home is not a concept outside of myself and that I must create it within—became a reality. I *am* home to these two girls and to my husband, their father, a simple state of fact that continues to unfold for me as each day passes.

This doesn't mean I don't struggle because of loss—that they will not have the joy of knowing their grandfathers, or that I can't look to Korea as more than my birthplace—those birth relatives, despite some serious searching, did not reveal themselves to me. Or that I don't have insecurities about being a mother and providing guidance and supporting my kids as they travel on their own journey—insecurities to which many parents can relate. It's just that the hills and valleys are so different now, based not on experiences all my own, but shaped for the faces of my daughters and carved by their adventures, struggles, and desires.

One day, I might tell them, *hills and valleys,* and who knows how they'll react? Maybe they'll roll their eyes with adolescent confidence, or shrug off my motherly advice as they forge their own paths. Maybe they'll take it to heart someday, like I did, or maybe they won't. And that's okay. Our landscape is made with our hearts and our souls, and our family is the horizon all around us.

It's Your Choice

Charlie Ritts

The days pass
each one with light
then dark
shadows across my
hands
I look better in the dark
and I force myself to
fall into a sleep
where I dream of a
woman called elle
who rode the el
and circles that are red
that circle a white pie-shaped cake
and of a wrinkly old man who
tells me to choose between
a pill:
Whole or crumbled?
it's your choice but
it will be significant

Yellow in the Bluegrass

Megan Brown

My ears are ringing with the lingering sounds of a concert when I see something sexy headed in my direction. My inner teenager suppresses a squeal as I realize it is a rock star who is lowering himself into the seat at the table I'm sharing with my friend Catherine. He begins to speak.

"Hello. My name is Kryz."

Who knew I was a sucker for brassy, foreign accents? His greeting slaps me in the brain, rendering me socially in-capable, and the adulation tumbling in my mind makes me dizzy. I wonder if all men are capable of looking this good in a camel-colored leather coat. He interrupts my thoughts and asks if he can guess where I'm from. I'm so starstruck I don't even care that he's using The Worst Pick Up Line For Asians Ever (TWPULFAE).

"Sure, go for it...Chris." *What kind of name is Kryz?*

"Are you from Japan?" *Not that my guess would be any better, but then, I've never resorted to TWPULFAE.*

"No."

"China?" *Why does no one ever guess Thailand?*

"No." *Any minute now process of elimination will kick in...*

"Korea?" *WINNER!!!* So he's not great at this game. This is fine because I'm still trying to pin down his accent, which I am pretty sure is either British or Australian. My friend Catherine is sitting beside me at least half a pint deep into her evening when she raises her drink to him, "You're IRISH aren't you?!" *Wow, she is good.*[1]

"Aye, from Dublin! D'ya like me waistcoat?" (I said I can't do accents, alright?) "What's a waistcoat?" He points to his vest. By now I am in full swoon over everything Kryz is saying. *Did he just say someone was "wackered?" Dreamy!*

Kryz asks me what my Korean name is, and I hesitate. I can never remember if it's Huang Yung Mi or Yung Mi Huang. I decide to just choose one (the wrong one, of course) and he murmurs back, "That's sexy."

No, Irishman—you are. I take a swig of Catherine's drink and nearly go blind from the amount of alcohol she has poured into it. Kryz goes to sign some autographs and as soon as he's out of earshot I blast Catherine with the wisdom of my fourth beer, "WHAT A CHARMING IRISH MAN. HE IS SUCH A BABE."

I feel guilty referring to him as a charming Irish man. Growing up a charming Asian lady, I know how it feels for someone to judge you solely on your country of origin, but here's the thing—I was drunk. I was drunk, and I grew up in a little, white town called Reidland which was made up of 98% Caucasians, 0.3% African Americans, 0.7% Asians, and 0% sweaty haired Irish men checking me out.[2]

You might wonder why there are twice the amount of Asians as there are African Americans in a small podunk town like Reidland. Me too; however, I have a theory. In my

1   I can't do accents for shit. Not even an Asian one.
2   Statistics courtesy of Wikipedia.

mind, the entire 0.7% of the Asian population in Reidland is comprised entirely of adopted children. There's this thing that Professor Eva Illouz calls "romanticization of commodities,"[3] which I think is responsible for this influx of Asian babies. Crudely put, romanticizing commodities is exactly what you think it is; it is why dinner on the table is a sign of a successful marriage. In short, it makes that disgusting box of chocolate covered cherries taste like anything other than the nauseating box of chocolates that it is. Maybe it's risky to say, but there is a "commodity" that no one ever mentions and that is children. Yes, a commodity. Set them atop your hip! Strap them to your back! Sling one under your arm and take it to the grocery. The only thing separating you from nosy neighbors that insinuate that your marriage reeks of failure is children. After all, they are the reason you have that hard-earned backyard and the only, ONLY reason you would ever buy a minivan. Babies! Everybody has to have one. Get yours today.

In all seriousness, I know it's not fair to attribute a theory of romanticized commodities to adoption. My mother's friend Cindy adopted out of love. But part of me secretly believes that her brood of all boys, no girls, was like having four gallons of milk, but no ice cream. If you had four boys and couldn't dream of pink onesies and prom dresses, would you blame Cindy for taking matters into her own hands? I didn't

---

3   *Consuming the Romatic Utopia: Love and the Cultural Contradictions of Capitalism* is a book by Professor Eva Illouz. All mentions of romanticization of commodities comes from *Chapter 1: Constructing the Romantic Utopia.* In her words, "The 'romanticization of commodities' refers to the way in which commodities acquired a romantic aura in early twentieth century movies and advertising imagery." (pg. 26) I have bastardized this theory to accommodate my feelings about adoption.

think so. Thus, when I was delivered from the airplane into my mother's arms, everyone immediately understood when Cindy turned to my mother with great conviction and said, "I know God wants me to adopt a child from Korea." And so, with God's stamp of approval, she followed my mother's lead and made a phone call to Holt International Children's Services to place an order for one female baby, no defects.

*

My parents made life easy on me. Unlike the made-for-TV drama that my peers thought I was experiencing, my parents never managed to pull the wool over my eyes that I was not their biological child. They were open about my adoption, telling me the airport story every night and even had a home movie of my arrival. They encouraged me to ask questions about Korea, but for a long time, I didn't have any. I told my mom, "I don't wonder about my biological mom because I think of you as my mom. I don't really wonder about Korea because I'm living here." It was just that simple to me.

A local adoption group, which my parents were a part of, saw cultural immersion as a more important activity than I ever did as a kid. The group tried relentlessly to interest all of its adoptees in Korean culture, taking us to diversity fairs and, once, an authentic Korean restaurant. As it turns out, five-year-old children do not want to eat a steamed pork dumpling when there is a McDonald's down the street. In the hands of children, multicultural, skin tone crayons, however politically correct, are just crayons.

When I was in fourth grade, the adoption group made a

great push for more Korean culture education. They arranged for Korean exchange students attending Murray State University to pair up with our families. We were supposed to spend time with them and learn about our culture firsthand, but I was not pleased with this arrangement. Cindy and her family loved their Korean, Kwan Jo, who was funny and outgoing, but my family was paired with Ji Young, who was less funny and annoyingly soft spoken. She once ate peanut butter and American cheese on the same cracker as I watched silently, trying to decide if I should feel humiliated for her or not. Ji Young had an accent that was thick with a sound I did not recognize. It was foreign in a way that "other" Asians were, not me. I felt foolish trying to communicate with her, constantly asking, "What?" She always wanted to hug me and talk to me, but I wanted to ignore her and read the *Sweet Valley Twins* series where they had sex and escaped homicidal lunatics.

My mom chided me, "Meg, just let her hug you. You probably remind her of home." "Fine, whatever." I let her hug me, but I didn't like it. Hugging Ji Young gave me a weird feeling. I knew that she was supposed to be "one of my people," but all I felt was utter disconnect.

*

I have felt disconnect like this for most of my life. When I was young, my mother would pick me up after school to take me to get my hair cut by Jo Tang. My mom liked Jo because she hailed from Thailand, and thus, knew how to properly cut Asian hair. I grew up most of my life with adult women grabbing my hair and saying, "I wish I had hair as nice as yours!" but I don't think they ever noticed that it felt like synthetic

Barbie hair. The nice thing about Jo was that she didn't praise my hair, she just hacked at it with a razor while she spoke rapid Thai into the cordless phone. The bad thing was that Jo made me feel uncomfortable the way Ji Young did. I would sit in the salon chair, raising and lowering my head at Jo's command, grateful that she wanted to talk to my mom about being a parent more than she wanted to talk to me about being Asian. To me, being Asian was an experience just short of having a disability, and Jo and I were crippled comrades, yellow people in a blue place. People cocked their heads like dogs solving long division then, asked tentatively, "So... does that mean your mom is Asian or your dad?"

Moments like these happened more than I cared for, especially in our elementary school cafeteria. The cafeteria was a hot bed of anxiety and soy meats that acted as a battleground for young, restless children. While sitting around Formica tables that smelled permanently of condiments and dishwater, we traded Jello and insults. "Are you PT?[4] Are you a virgin? Are you gay?[5]" But I was the only one being asked, "Do you know how to speak Korean? Why not? Do you remember your mom?" Many times, I would forget how old I was when I was shipped to the U.S. and I felt embarrassed that I could not remember this essential fact about myself. I definitely did not know anything about my birth, and I wasn't clever enough to make up a cool story.

I imagine lunch line was torture for all adopted kids, as it

---

4   If yes, PT stands for "pregnant teenager"; if no, PT stands for "potty-trained."

5   Don't worry, it wasn't really about being virginal or gay. We just wanted to haze each other for our lack of wordly knowledge.

was an excellent place for forcing everyone to celebrate your birthday with you. Some kids used great precision, "Happy birthday, Lindsey!"

"Oh, it's not my birthday yet. It will be at 11:09 a.m. though."

Some boasted about their mothers' ability to endure pain. "My mom was in labor with me for twelve hours! My brother took two days! And now she's pregnant again!"

Others had namesakes. "I was named after my grandma. Her middle name is Elizabeth, too!"

My mother had named me after Meg from *Little Women*, but who the hell cared about *Little Women*? I knew Meg wasn't the badass writer; she wasn't the one who burned the writer's manuscript, and she wasn't even the one who died. Meg was a BORING character from a boring book. I stayed quiet during birthday conversations hoping no one would ask me anything. Not only did I know absolutely nothing about my birth, but I had a weird middle name leftover from my parents' and older brother's sense of humor. Because it would have actually been cruel to name me, "Mi Yung Megan Brown" (Me! Young Megan Brown!) they settled for keeping "Yung" to preserve my heritage. Sure, it's not the worst thing that can happen to you, but when you're in elementary school, "Yung" is never a one-word story. It's an explanation.

Lucky for me, I was not the only one that lunch line was hard on. During elementary school lunch line, the slow moving snake of restless children compensated for its boredom by creating cruel games to torture everybody. Cooties were a third grade favorite. There was one boy in our class who was deemed so repulsive that everyone started circling and dotting their arms with cootie shots as soon as he came near. Passing his cooties happened so frequently that it soon became a full blown epidemic. Our stern, white-haired teacher, Mrs. Blythe, put an end to our vicious game and seized the opportunity for a much needed lesson in tolerance. From that point on, anyone caught spreading anyone else's cooties had to write an apology note.

I never received any apology notes, but I still imagined there were a lot of Megan Brown cooties going around. I was unpopular, but I was hoping it was only because my mother had a thing for bows. Homemade bows made out of ribbon from the fabric shop and hot glued to a clip. Purple and silver shoelace bows. Little flags atop my head proclaiming, "Different!" Pink bows. Red bows. Every day.

Despite the bows, I managed to snag myself a boyfriend in third grade. Brad was a total embarrassment, yelling, "See you tomorrow, pretty woman!" as I rushed to the bus after school. I wasn't sure if it was the bows or Brad, but something was making me a huge loser. My grades certainly did not help. I would get teased for scoring 100s on tests, so I finally decided that something had to go. Because there are certain things about being a third grade girl that you can get away with without so much judgment, I decided to sabotage my grades.

I stared at my math tests, "4 X 8 = ___" I penciled in 32, thought better of it, erased, and wrote 31. Totally believable. I was careful to miss only a few problems here and there as to not arouse suspicion, but it wasn't long before Stacy Denton and her sassy third grade mouth blurted out, "I BET YOU MISSED THOSE ON PURPOSE!" My face flushed the same Sharpie red as the 90 written at the top of my test. Was it embarrassing to be smart? Or was it embarrassing to be a smart Asian?

*

Over the years, I learned that being Asian did have a few perks. I got made fun of for having good grades, but I realized this wasn't as bad as having the grossest cooties or throwing up in class. As I got older, I learned that being Asian meant playing a certain role in life. You were assigned the part of the calculator-smart sex symbol that rarely spoke or the calculator-smart sex symbol with dragon-lady ferocity. It really didn't seem so bad in comparison to the racist things said about other people. I mean, you got to be sexy, right?

I felt conflicted that one could have racism for one group of people and not another. I wondered if I was really an exception to the people I loved or if they didn't think about my race at all. I figured that if my own friends and family could joke about race the way they did, then no one actually meant to be racist; it was just an innocent mistake and one that I could readily excuse. After all, wasn't talking about race full of mistakes? Once, I got asked, "Honey what *kind* are you?" Another time, a friend confessed to me that he had told someone, "Duhhhhh, her last name is Brown... like her skin!"[6] I didn't even know myself that "Oriental" is a word only applicable to rugs and trading companies, never people. No one is ever

---

6   I bet Amy Tan got that one all of the time.

really good at talking about race, but I'd like to have faith that we are all trying.

*

I'm going to let you in on a little secret about race. If you're uncomfortable talking about race, try making it delicious. Chances are you'll never be rude enough to say, "Hey, slant eyes," but "almond shaped" is totally fair game. If you read any book featuring characters that are not Caucasian, you will notice they all have mocha, coffee, or olive colored skin. It might actually be the only way to tastefully (pun intended) describe other people. If in doubt, try a non-food comparison and see if it sounds right to you. Go ahead. "Her skin was the color of stain resistant khakis." Right.[7]

So why is the relationship between food and race so important to me? During college, food and race were my introduction to a new catalog of racially inappropriate terms. In my women's studies class, I learned what it meant to be a "Twinkie" or a "banana." A girl in my class explained, "You know...yellow on the outside, white on the inside..." Oh, like the Asian version of an Oreo. I get it.

I felt like I should have been offended on some higher level that disapproved of this sort of slang, but what I didn't realize was that offensive slang would become the only way I could think through my feelings. "Weeaboo"[8] described that

---

7   Still afraid of making a racial faux pas? Stick to dessert flavors, e.g., cinnamon, ginger, butterscotch, cream, caramel, honey, molasses, milk, nutmeg, toffee. Vegetables, proteins, and grain just don't have the same ring, e.g., potato, cooked steak, squashes and gourds, oatmeal, rye, beer.

8   Urban Dictionary describes a "weeaboo" as someone who is overly enthusiastic for the Japanese culture. I also learned that this term can be substituted for "wapanese."

dopey kid from high school with the bad bowl cut. "Fob"[9] explained the way I felt when I saw other Asian people and compared their Asian-ness to my own. Though I didn't know it at the time, fob also described my discomfort towards Ji Young. And now there was "Twinkie" or "banana" to describe the way I had felt my whole life. I didn't find the slang offensive, I found it necessary. It's important to have words to describe how you feel, even if you have to keep them to yourself.

Around the time I learned about Twinkies and bananas, I realized that it is also important to have biological parents. It just hit me one day; no one had ever told me, "You have your mother's nose." I had no visual indicator of my future and no amusing food words were going to soothe the ache that growing up without a parental crystal ball caused. Was I going to have white hair or grey hair? When would the wrinkles start!? I needed to know: To what degree is the body flexible? Or is it all static, written permanently on the genes?

My therapist once asked, "Growing up, did you feel different?" But I told her, "No, it wasn't bad. I mean there were other Asian people, but you know. It was alright." But it wasn't alright. Everything was wrong—my feet, my hair, my butt, my boobs, my face, my everything was wrong. I was unsure if this was my fault or nature's fault. I had never spent this much time before worrying about being Asian. Sure, I had had some uncomfortable experiences, but it would have been stupid to continue fretting over something so unchangeable. So instead of dwelling on my Asian issues, I worried about everything else. I worried about recycling, making sure

9   Fob is an acronym for "fresh off the boat." I guess that means when
      I was a baby, I was a fop—"fresh off the plane."

to put the frozen food boxes in the green bin and the cereal boxes in the blue one; I worried about my relationship with my boyfriend (in shambles), homework (always too much), and my health. I was so sure I was a case of fibromyalgia, Lyme disease, or diabetes, but of course, I had none of them. I had many unanswered questions, and I was only certain of two things; one—my depression had nothing to do with being Asian, and two—maybe it had something to do with my parents, (isn't it always parents?), but it was definitely not because I was Asian. I knew I was being crazy but I did not want to stop.

*

"Well, if you don't think it's about being Asian, what do you think it's about?" "I don't know. I mean, I'm just depressed. My depression makes me feel this way." "But where does that depression come from?" "Aren't I paying you to figure that out?" I didn't actually say the last thing, but I was frustrated that we seemed to be going in circles. My therapist and I had many exchanges like this where she would probe gently and I would shut down. She would approach the topic of being Asian and I would steer us down a path of "Mom said this..." or "Dad said that...," ex-boyfriends, and suicidal friends. I bitched and cried my way through entire boxes of Kleenex twisting them into my hands until they came apart in soggy, white pellets.

I'm hardly qualified to make claims about the powers of repression, but I do know that the more I reflected on being Asian, the more my depression lifted. I can't ignore the coincidence. Being in therapy was like opening a matryoshka and finding a hundred tiny dolls all stuck inside each other, yellow on the outside, white on the inside.

I think that people forget to acknowledge the importance in making a distinction between the inside and the outside. I don't think people always recognize the transparent boundary that lies between the banana peel and the fruit flesh. The first time you hurt someone's feelings, you realize you have to hold on just a little bit tighter to some words so that they don't slide past your lips. You learn that some things stay inside. For me, being Asian was one of those inside things. For others, it was an outside thing that could be grabbed, laughed about, and quickly dismissed. Sometimes people forget that race is not temporary. It is not a yearbook photo with braces or a perm. You do not grow out of it. You grow into it like a training bra and then, if everything goes okay, you grow up.

*

"So, I need to get back to the tour bus. I'd like to get your number."

I know I am one of many the rockstar will charm. I tap my number into his phone and he tells me to make a sultry face for a picture. *Sultry?* His camera-phone whirs, capturing the pinched look of my suppressed laughter. I tell him he should try to remember me.

"Of course I'll remember ya!" he says as he types into his phone, "You're the h-o-t- K-o-r..." I begin to flinch, but I stop. *You're one hell of a looker*, I think, *you're a charming Irish man.*

KimPab Stories

Kim WoongJee DeGraaf

Never a lonely seoul in DAEGU.
When I'm a staying alone in seoul
my heart feels like an empty hole,
So I bust out the music within me
beat walkin' to my girl Amerie
Jammin' down these busy streets like a stranger,
but I don't need a partner, I'm not the lone ranger
I'll never need tanto, cuz you don't fear danger
when you're rockin' alone in the manger.

Sooooo, I gotta get up and eat some kimpab,
gotta stay persistent in finding a job,
won't ever stay down, lazy or bored,
cuz' I'm an mvp like my boy Hines Ward.
I'm going back to Daegu to see my Noona
" 왜ㅐㅐㅐ", cuuuz 나는 고아 사람 입니다 와
{"Waeeee", cuuuz NaNeun KoA SaRam IbNiDa, Wa}
("why y y y", cuuuz I'm an orphaned person, and)
A young orphan from Korea
never worries about, having no ma or pa.

Soooo, I build up the courage and take the Subway.

I'm too tired and excited like it's may,

So I'll bust out the Amerie cd and I'll be okay.

Make sure I run through these people like Hines Ward all day.

I'm in Daegu at YeongNam University.

You see, all the students want to see me

when I'm in Daegu city, I'm a hometown hero, Hyung & Oppa

and I'm never a lonely soul in DAEGU, with all my friends and NooNa.

고맙다 (Ko Mab Da) I'll see all of ya'll word up!!!

How It All Turned Out

Judy Eckerle

Date: Thu, 26 Oct 2006 17:09:14 -0700 (PDT)
From: kyung rim (judy)
Subject: how it all turned out

Dear Friends:

I met the people claiming to be my birth family on the morning before my flight back to the United States. There were four people there. The first one to walk into the room took my breath away. She was tall with freckles and slightly wavy hair like mine. All I could think was that this was actually happening. Then three people walked in behind her who were short, heavyset, and had round faces. Hmmm. My translator explained that the three people were the possible birth sister, brother, and mother. The only person in the room that looked like me was the brother's fiancé. Let me just say that there have never been three people who looked more like each other *and* looked nothing like me. I think we all knew what the outcome would be, but we talked for a while, the birth mother crying the whole time and intently studying my face as if she could will some part of me to look like her. They were lovely, well-intentioned people with sadness in their eyes.

The condensed story is that the birth mother was not married to the father when she had the baby. Her brother, feeling that she had "shamed" the family, took the baby after she was born and gave her to an agency for adoption. The birth mother says that she walked for miles and going to all the agencies she could the next day—but never found the baby.

She later married that birth father, and they had three more children together. She told the oldest child, a daughter, about the adoption about ten years ago and that birth sister started to search for her older sister. About seven years ago, she read an article about me on the Internet and contacted the author, who told her I wasn't ready to meet them but he would tell me about them, so they have been "waiting" for me to meet them for almost seven years. That contact was later identified as a man in a Korean prison who had stalked me for months some time earlier when there were numerous TV and newspaper articles about my search. As crazy as that was, I never knew he was also claiming to be my contact. Is it possible he knows about other people who have contacted him? Crazy. You can't even make this stuff up. The sister then found another article about my search with the contact number of an actual friend and led us to this.

When we took the DNA tests, the birth mother held my hands and cried while she said over and over how she had looked for me, how she had thought of me every day. That the birth father was so overcome with emotion he made himself sick and couldn't even come with them that morning. I told her that even if she turned out not to be my birth mother, that I had always wanted to hear the words of a birth mother that wanted her baby, that I had always wondered if birth mothers think of their children and that I was grateful to her for sharing with me. I told her that I had the best life possible and that I was thankful for having been adopted. She wept and said that she felt peaceful for the first time in thirty years.

We all hugged goodbye, already knowing in our hearts that we were not the same family. I was about to go to bed one night in America about two weeks later when I checked my email and found, as I suspected, the news from my agency that the DNA tests were not a match.

I am at peace. It would have been incredibly complicated to have gone down the other path. Maybe all of this happened just to give a little solace to a birth mother who is still grieving her loss—thirty years later. Maybe it was to tell me not to give up because you never know what is around to corner. What-ever it is, I'm moving on and I'm grateful for it all.

Thanks again for your emails and prayers and good thoughts.

Much love,
Judy

Likeability

Sandra Gibbons

"Why are you so happy all the time?" I've been asked that a lot. Of course I am not happy all the time, but I am bizarrely incapable of showing stress and my less amiable emotions in front of most people. I've never tried explaining my cheerful personable disposition to anyone, including myself. But recently, what began as a simple debate over one racist remark ended in enlightenment on the matter of my character. My self-psychological profiling has managed to fascinate me.

* * *

After two failed attempts at having biological children, in February 1977 my parents decided to adopt a seven-month-old baby girl from Korea. That was me. My mom was a Polish beautician and my father a German banker. Home was a house in the suburbs of Detroit, Michigan, where I lived until I was twenty-five years old. I was surrounded by all the right things—love, happiness, family, friends, and financial stability. A kid could not have asked for more. I was my parents' blessing, and they were my saving grace.

Where there's light, there are shadows. And as a child, shadows always seem scarier when you don't know what's causing them. In the late '70s and through the '80s, racial diversity existed in Metro-Detroit, but was fractured into segregated communities. Racism seemed to exist in every community. Though it primarily revolved around black and white prejudices, I was too young to understand the finer points of cultural and socioeconomic differences as I began to learn about such issues. I understood the existence of biases against skin color, and I knew I wasn't white. I rarely saw anyone who wasn't Caucasian in my neighborhood. We lived in an overwhelmingly white demographic. I was a novelty to myself and to those around me. I looked Asian, but that was the only Asian thing about me.

People of course, were curious. For me, the term, "icebreaker" meant the question, "What nationality are you?" (I found it amusing when I learned my nationality is in fact, American.) I have been approached and greeted in Asian languages. It is assumed I am book-smart and know martial arts. I have heard several comments about how funny it was for a 4'9" Asian to be working in an Italian restaurant. I have fumbled with self-conscious feelings when people told me (when I was young) that I looked just like a china doll and (as I got older) how beautiful Asian women are. These have all been in large part innocent, but also constant reminders I am not Caucasian. When I was young and insecure (as most children are), it was a constant reminder I did not fit in.

For every one racial slur I heard growing up, I probably remember hearing five. I grew quickly and achingly aware that people judge each other by skin color. I decided people were biased against this, and I saw unfriendliness where perhaps there was none. I heard rejection where it did not exist. When I was about ten years old, I was riding my bike in the neighborhood when a kid came running after me yelling

"Hey! Chinese lady!" I pedaled frantically away thinking angrily, "I'm not Chinese!" I was certain his graceless approach was an indication that what would follow would be unpleasant. Despite the dismay I recall with such clarity, I realize now he was probably trying to tell me I dropped my sunglasses or ask me if I had a quarter.

When I was 11 years old, a boy joked he could blindfold me with dental floss and a small group of kids around us laughed. While every kid is the target of a mean joke at some point, that one damaged my self-image for a ridiculously long time. I remember wanting surgery on my eyes to make me look less Asian. As I got older, I learned about Hitler and white supremacists, of racial slurs like "gook" and "chink," and that somewhere along the way America had been involved in a war with North Korea. All these things made me uncomfortable in my own skin.

I was determined I would not be disliked, judged, or stereotyped based on my race. I was sadly terrified I would be pigeon-holed into a hole I didn't like. Never mind most people around me held little to no negative biases against Asians. Like every other kid I set out to prove myself. But I was proving my likeability. I went out of my way to be friendly and charming, make eye contact, and smile a lot. If I knew you for longer than a half hour, I hugged you. I talk to people and open up to them. And people like me. You know how positive reinforcement works. It all became a large part of me. Fortunately, those reasons no longer drive the rosy disposition.

I was about 19 or 20 when I embraced my Korean heritage. Suddenly I felt starved to learn about Korea—its culture and people. At age thirty-three, I returned to South Korea for the first time and cannot begin to describe what a profoundly extraordinary trip it was in every aspect. While I enjoyed the feeling of not being a minority, I of course could not ignore the fact I was a minority to Korean culture.

This is exactly where I belong. Very rarely do I ever feel self-conscious about my heritage anymore. I love celebrating and learning about Korean culture, especially since my visit there. There are so many reasons why I am a sincerely happy person; I have an incredible husband, two perfect little boys, parents who loved me (more than I could understand until I became a parent myself), and amazing friends and family. I live in the United States where many of its citizens work relentlessly to end racism and the often irreparable damage it so often causes. I am incredibly blessed to have all these things in my life as well as the realization to be grateful for them all.

It is satisfying to finally have an answer to the question, "Why are you so happy all the time?" I've enjoyed sharing this, and I hope that it helps to spark your own inward reflection. Self-discovery is not only intriguing, but fulfilling—and it is certainly one of those roads which can lead to genuine happiness.

Art

Kayla Tange

Untitled

Josiah Bell

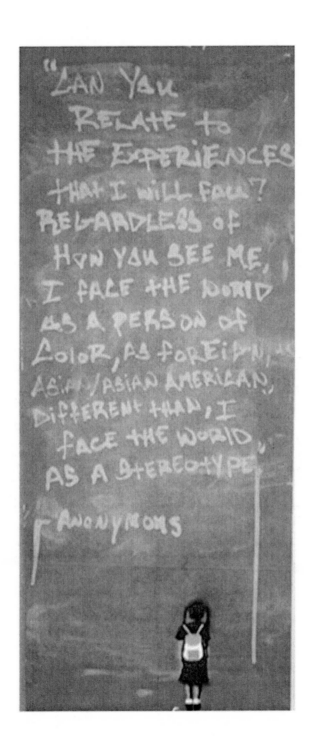

Orchid

Jessica Emmett

My birthmother's name was Thi Lan, which I was told means "pretty orchid" in Vietnamese. The number etched into the orchid was the refugee number that she was given when arriving in Hong Kong after fleeing Vietnam after the war. The number cannot be used to trace due to a lack of records at that time. This is the second piece in my flower series.

Misplaced Baggage—
Same, Same But Different

Anh Dao Kolbe

Adoption Experience— Escaping the Rain

Elizabeth Mehaffey

Art

Renee Meyer Ernst

Art

Renee Meyer Ernst

Names

Kim Tobin King

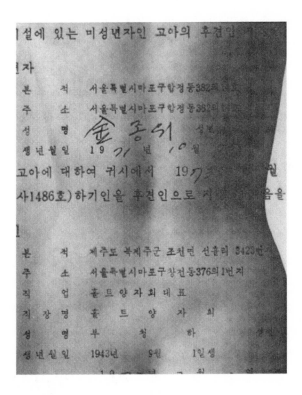

When I was born, I was presumably given a name. I was called that name for the first 15 months of my life. Then one January day in Seoul, I was left crying on a street corner; abandoned. I was found, but my name was lost forever.

After that January day, I was given a new Korean name and identification number and then yet another "American" name when I was adopted several months later.

As a young woman I often daydreamed of returning to that street corner hoping to hear my name whispered to me by the ghosts of my ancestors. And when they whispered my name I would somehow begin to remember who I was and understand everything that had happened to me.

I spent a large part of my life telling myself I didn't need to know. It didn't matter... I wasn't that child anymore. I started to believe I didn't care.

The other day I heard a snippet on the car radio in between the singing and bickering of my girls in the back seat. The story was about how when we pass, we die three times. First is when your body dies, the second is when you are buried, and the third is when your name is spoken for the last time. I don't know what they were referring to or whom the quote was attributed to, but for a moment in time all I heard was silence and my heart grieved again for that little girl sitting on the street crying. I wondered if her name, my name, had been spoken for the last time or if there was someone still keeping my memory alive.

The name I cherish the most—no matter how overused—sent me crashing back to reality. "MOMMY! EMME WON'T LET ME SING!" I wiped my eyes and looked up into the rear view mirror and smiled at my girls. It was then I decided to stop trying to bury that little girl in me. I do care, and even though I cannot speak her name, she is a part of me and I will keep her alive. She is no longer a child, a victim; she has grown into a woman, a wife, and a mother. For now, that will have to be enough.

Seoul Searching

Brian Conyer

Monday, August 24th had arrived. This was the day I was to encounter blood relatives for the first time in over twenty-four years. I met with Sue, my social worker, at the social service office in the morning and then together we headed to Seoul Station to depart for the three hour train ride to Busan, South Korea. The train ride was calm and emotionless. My expectations were low and my curiosity was slight. Maybe it was the chaotic schedule leading up to this moment. My mind was too busy to take a moment to realize what I was about to encounter. Or maybe my mind was simply preparing itself for what I was about to experience. Regardless, I wasn't sure what to expect.

The train arrived in Busan at 12:30 p.m. I turned off my iPod, and Sue softly said to me that my aunt would greet us at the gates and take us to her home where my birth father and grandmother awaited. This kept my anticipation to a minimum since it would just be my aunt at the station. Sue and I rode the escalators up to the lobby floor, and she looked around for a woman who could potentially be my relative. I just looked around with a blank stare, having no clue what to look for or what to expect.

As we approached a set of gates exiting the terminal, I was bombarded by five individuals with eyes that were bright red and filled with tears. Three women in the group immediately ran to me, grabbing my face, pulling on my arms and hands, repeatedly saying a phrase I could not understand. I was in shock and overwhelmed. I stared at the ground because it was impossible for me to look any of these strangers in the eyes. My heart was racing, my chest feeling like it was about to explode. My mind focused only on Sue's words as it was the only familiar voice I could hear. She shouted to me above the foreign words, "this is your uncle, this is your aunt, this is your grandmother, this is your other aunt."

As I finally made my first attempt to look up and capture the faces of the people she was naming, I locked eyes with a man at the back of the group who was a bit standoffish. I immediately saw an image of myself thirty years in the future. Instantly I knew that this man was my birth father. Sue must have seen the bewilderment in my eyes because she quickly grabbed the man and brought him to me saying, "This is your birth father." Instantly, I lost control of my breathing and burst into irrepressible tears. I hadn't cried like this since I was fourteen years old when my dog died. I had never experienced such confusion in my head and what felt like a thousand pound weight on my chest. I backed away from the group needing my own space in an attempt to recollect myself. Not only did I fail to resist the emotions that overtook me, but I failed to escape from my relatives. They chased me, grabbed me, making me feel even more uncomfortable. Not knowing what to do, I gave up trying to create space for myself and allowed them to bombard me.

Things began to slow down. Several minutes passed and I still struggled to make eye contact. Sue suggested that we leave the train station, sensing how overwhelmed and uncomfortable I was. We headed to a restaurant for our next destination where the family had reserved a private room. My birth father and uncle led the way, Sue followed close behind, and I walked in the very back unwillingly holding hands with my two aunts and my grandmother gripping my shirt. Unable to think clearly, I kept my head down as we walked to the car, staring aimlessly at the ground and asking what had I got myself into.

After a short car ride, we arrived at a buffet style restaurant. We were seated in a back room around a very large rectangular table where everyone just sat there and stared at me. In an attempt not to be the center of attention, I sat at the corner of the table. As I prepared myself to address the family for the first time, an aunt that I had not met burst into the room like a scene out of a movie. She ran straight to me grabbing my hands as she fell to her knees with tears streaming down her face. I avoided looking in the eyes, trying to keep the composure that I had just regained. Even though I knew it was rude, I did not acknowledge her presence at my feet because I did not want to lose control of my emotions again. After several long minutes she got back on to her feet, smiled, and sat directly across from me.

In my second attempt to begin conversation, I told the family that I had come back to Korea to thank them. To thank them for giving me up for adoption, as it was the best decision for me. I told them I was happy and was raised by the most amazing parents who gave me ample opportunities to assure my happiness. I told them that I did not want them to live with any regret for giving me up for adoption because I did not live with regret for being adopted. No one seemed to be able to find anything to say, but simply smiled at me with a slight look of appreciation and also confusion.

As if I were a child, my relatives affectionately forced me to try a variety of foods and watched me until I ate every last bite on the plate. Lunch finally ended and I was stuffed. Our next destination was one of my aunt's nearby apartment. The emotions among the group had shifted from a sense of guilt and sadness, to light and cheerful. On the way to the apartment I began telling jokes to show my lighthearted side. My grandmother told me that when she was much younger and stronger she would carry me everywhere on her back. I put my arm around her shoulders and playfully replied that if it would make her feel better I would let her carry me on her back on our walk to the car.

The rest of the afternoon we sat on the apartment floor around a table that was filled with an array of fruits for snacking. During this time my uncle's wife and two daughters arrived along with another one of my cousins. We drank beer and told stories about our current lives. The living room was filled with chatter, and even though I could not understand what was being said, I enjoyed observing how affectionately everyone interacted. For the most part, I quietly sat there admiring how close they were as a family. I could always tell when the topic of conversation was me because someone from the family would briefly stop the conversation, make eye contact with me, and then look at the group for some type of confirmation as they resumed their dialogue.

Interaction at this point was effortless although Sue had to translate everything. They tried to compare the features of my face to their memories of me as a baby. They joked that I no longer had double eyelids, but that I still had the same eyes and nose from when I was a child. They noted my gray hairs, but said I still had a baby face. They commented that like my birth father, I smile with my eyes. And on and on they continued. I don't think I've ever been analyzed so much for so long, but I didn't mind. Although I was in a similar position, I couldn't imagine what they were experiencing to see me twenty-four years later.

The time came for Sue and me to head back to Seoul. The family pleaded for me to spend the night. I selfishly declined the offer as I was emotionally drained. I wanted things to slow down and to absorb what I had just experienced in solitude. However, we agreed to stay for dinner. After dinner was over, they again begged for us to stay another hour. Sue convinced me that it would be best if we stay for a while longer to please my birth family. The hour quickly passed, and they asked for us to stay late into the night and catch the last train to Seoul. Exhausted, I told Sue that I felt bad that she had to stay so long and I thought it was best for us to leave. The family agreed to take us to the train station to catch the 9 p.m. train, three and a half hours past our original reservations.

We arrived at the train station and said our goodbyes. Surprisingly it started off fairly easy. Sue and I marched down the line of family members saying our goodbyes with smiles and hugs. Waiting for me at the end of the line was my tiny, old, toothless grandmother. As I slowly approached her, I could tell that this goodbye was going to be the most difficult for her. Tears quickly filled her eyes, and she grabbed my shirt and buried her face into my chest. She looked up at me, staring deep into my eyes and said something that I could not understand. I looked to Sue for a translation, but tears began to run down her face as well. I asked her what my grandmother said to make her cry, and she replied, "Your grandmother says that she is very old and feels that she is close to dying and her last wish in life is for you to come back so she can see you once more before she dies." I immediately looked into my grandmother's eyes and nodded yes. She relieved her grip on me and backed away.

I gave a final wave and smile to everyone and boarded the train. I took my seat and looked outside, surprised to see everyone still lined up watching my departure. Realizing I was unsure if I could actually keep the promise I just made my grandmother—from a mixture of guilt, confusion, and selfishness, I began to cry. Sue consoled me as the train left the station, and within five minutes of leaving, I fell asleep for the entire ride back to Seoul.

The Good Eater and
Other Food Thoughts

Mary Lee Vance

Having passed the 50 year mile marker years ago, I have begun to realize that being older has its advantages. In this case my advantage is that I am one of a few Korean adoptees left who had the good fortune of personally knowing both Harry and Bertha Holt, founders of Holt International, who nearly single handedly spearheaded intercountry adoption. Today hardly anyone bats an eye at the concept of international adoption, but back in the late 1950s and early 1960s, such occurrences were rare and certainly newsworthy.

I was "discovered" by Mr. Holt when I was in the Seoul Baby Hospital, where I had apparently been taken after a police officer supposedly found me abandoned and alone. However, my childhood memories of the event were that I had been deliberately taken to the hospital for medical care by my birth family, as I had contracted polio and they were unable to care for me. (Later, when I met my birth mother, this story of mine was verified.)

During the post Korean War period, children of mixed races and with disabilities were destined for miserable lives. They were not socially accepted, and at most could only hope to survive in the poorest of conditions. Not surprisingly, Mr. Holt made it a mission to have me adopted and sent to the

States, despite opposition from the nurses and administrators of the Baby Hospital. In fact, he already had an adoptive family lined up that was willing to take me, but first he had to gain custody of me before the Korean government would release me for overseas adoption.

Mr. Holt thought I would be better off in the States, while the Korean hospital personnel were afraid that I would be mistreated if sent outside the country. Furthermore, the Korean hospital administration intimated that I might be mentally retarded, and they were even more concerned about my safety because of this possible complication. However, American and Canadian nurses at the hospital were indignant that I would be identified as possibly retarded, stating that I "was one of the brightest children there."

In order to prevent me from leaving the country, the Korean hospital administrators lodged a complaint against Mr. Holt at the American Consul and threatened him with jail when they learned Mr. Holt wanted to have me adopted. Among other traits, Mr. Holt was stubborn, and continued to push for my hospital release into his custody. Finally after much wrangling, Mr. Holt was able to extricate me from the hospital and take me back to his room, where I stayed for some time before being mainstreamed into Nok Bun Dong orphanage while awaiting adoption. In a letter to my adoptive parents he wrote, "When I took her from the hospital it was cold. She had nothing but a nightgown, didn't even have pants. I wrapped her in my coat to take her home."

When it became evident that I would soon be adopted, a former American hospital nurse wrote to my adoptive parents.

"She is a fat little darling and with those heavy braces, she was more than I should have lifted. My heart ached leaving her. Now I know she will be well taken care of. It will take time before she laughs and talks—she just looks out of those big black eyes. And, she loved to eat!"

Later Mr. Holt would write to my adoptive parents about my stay at the hospital. "They have taken good care of your little girl Myung Ja. She is a little too fat, but outside of that she has just come along fine and she is a lovely child. I have fallen in love with her." He then added. "She has been staying in my room, as I say, and she is really a go-getter. She has practically worn me to a frazzle. She laughs and plays and gets into everything in my room, but I really enjoy her and I pray for her daily, in fact several times a day, that God will provide for her, and it is his will that she be your little daughter. I am sure he will perform it some way."

After I was "rescued," Mr. Holt had me examined. The Korean doctor decreed I was "plump" and a "good eater." Soon thereafter I got measles and TB. Adoption was delayed until a clean bill of health was reached.

While in the orphanage, I was fed well and continued to be a good eater. Pictures of me at the time show me sitting somberly with little shriveled legs, big potbelly, and large dark eyes observing the photographer. On June 3, 1961, I entered the United States and landed in Portland, Oregon, and began a life of food obsession in the land of plenty.

My earliest memories of the States involved food. I loved any kind of vegetable and fruits, but preferred them mostly raw. This preference made sense when I met my maternal grandmother nearly four decades later. I learned from her that I had spent my first couple years with her and had spent much of my time playing in her garden. With a smile on her lips, my maternal grandmother confirmed something that did not surprise me. She said, "You were a good eater."

However while I loved fruits and veggies, I did not like meat, and to this day do not like meat very much, opting for vegetarian cuisine most of the time. A favorite family memory of my brother and sister was when I was sitting alone at the dining table one night, after having refused to eat my now congealed meat entrée with the rest of the family at the table. Suddenly I had a bright idea, I would carefully bite and chew my meat, and then spit the meat into my napkin. Then, I would throw away my napkin, and everyone would think I had finished my dinner. The plan worked up until I threw away my napkin. Unbeknownst to me, the waste container had been emptied, so when I threw away the napkin, it made a loud sound when it landed. To this day, my nieces and nephews know the story well, as it was clearly told to them by my brother and sister frequently, and they all still think it is very funny.

Many times while growing up I would argue with my parents that I did not want to eat certain things (like meat), and they would insist that I eat whatever was on my plate. Several times I would challenge them and say, "Look at me, do I look undernourished?" To which they would respond, "Eat."

And yet, I was plagued by my weight. My polio-weakened legs couldn't handle my body weight, and eventually I had to wear not only full leg braces, but also use crutches and an electric scooter. Vainly I tried to diet to ease the pressure on my legs, but then ultimately gave up as the next food temptation kicked me back into food sensory overload.

Food continued to be both a delight and a challenge to me all my life. Growing up, I loved McDonald's fries and got excited whenever there were potlucks and dinners out. My mother kept a full fridge, cupboards, and freezer, so I never knew hunger. There was always something to eat, and always something I could make to eat.

As a teenager, I was plagued with all the usual insecurities, including bad skin, bloated body, and ugly sense of inferiority. It is not difficult to imagine my sense of self esteem being thoroughly poor when I met Mrs. Holt at a Korean adoptee gathering in my state. While I didn't mind meeting her, what I did mind was being told to stand by her and the other cute little Korean adoptees (I was the oldest and ugliest one present), to pose for a newspaper picture. The picture appeared on the front page of the paper the next day and shows me scowling as I towered over the other adoptees (who were cute as buttons).

After I moved out of my parents' house, I continued to feel great comfort in food. I needed to have full refrigerators, freezers, and cupboards too. I learned how to bake and freeze foods so I would always have something ready to eat and ready to serve in case company stopped by. I taught myself to dry food and do other food preparations. I hosted numerous potlucks where I did much of the cooking in advance, so that there would be enough variety of flavors and colors. I was a food pack rat and food obsessed. I loved to collect and give away food.

In college I became the menu coordinator for international student dinners so I could learn how to cook more foods, and I became a collector of different spices and ways to prepare a variety of dishes. I became in essence even more obsessive about food, and all the many ethnic ways one could prepare a certain kind of food product, like lentils or rice.

My hunger for food did not stop with eating or preparation. I collected cookbooks, and read them endlessly, and learned how to discuss food preparations with others. I even taught a freshman seminar course on nonwestern food culture, where I showed food theme movies, discussed food topics such as dining traditions around the world, and brought in food samples that I had prepared. I did cooking demonstrations in my home and elsewhere. I worked for a food service company, and for a while I made eggrolls for a deli.

The food obsessions started to make sense for the first time when I went to my first Korean Adoptee Gathering in D.C. I soon learned that most of the KADs of my age were similarly obsessed with food, not necessarily to my level, but they all enjoyed food shopping, and felt best when they were surrounded by food.

Years later I met Koreans who were able to enlighten me on the food fixation. They informed me that to be a "good eater" as a child meant that the child was in essence going to be a survivor. For a child to not want to eat, it meant the child was giving up on life. Since I loved food and ate it with enjoyment, to the point I even got competitive to get my share,

I survived my childhood in Korea and was able to survive my childhood in the States. I did not turn away from food, and in essence did not give up on life.

So, although for a long time references to me being a good eater bothered me, I slowly began to accept the comments for what they were, observations related to survivors. Yes I was overweight all my life, but I wasn't exactly morbidly obese or anything. Nonetheless it concerned me that Koreans felt a compulsion to observe what I ate, and that somehow my eating patterns were an issue. Yet when I met my birth family and was able to eat all the Korean food set in front of me, I felt a strange sense of pride in this accomplishment when I saw their smiles of approval.

Along with my enjoyment of food came my appreciation for research and for learning. As a result, I was able to work full time at Michigan State University as an academic advisor and liaison for Asian Pacific American students, while also working on my doctorate part-time.

In 1994 I earned my doctorate, and got a wonderful surprise in the mail, a handwritten letter from (Grandma) Bertha Holt. She did not mention food, or my eating patterns, but did note that she was proud of my goal achievement and that she "knew it was a struggle but you won it."

Eventually I became a food writer for *Korean Quarterly*, and still write articles pulling from my Midwest background and food fusion experiments. I now had better understanding about why it was actually a good thing to be known as a "good eater," and did not view it as a negative, or as a struggle. It was simply now just a part of who I am, a part of my identity.

Today I use a motorized scooter everywhere I go on campus, in my roles as a student services administrator, a profession that I have held since 1984. I have a Ph.D. from Michigan State University, have published in referred journals and in textbooks, and been the lead editor for two books, with a third one in progress. My husband of 30+ years has been with me through my entire professional career, and supportive of my passions (and obsessions) related to food and other topics. None of this would have happened had I not been a good eater, been hungry to learn, and ultimately been adopted to the States.

So I realize now that starting in life, as a good eater has been a good thing for me. As a proud member of Group One, the oldest group at the First International Gathering in D.C., I later observed at the 2004 Korea Gathering that we were the "oldies but goodies." We are survivors of life's circumstances. Those of us who eat, survive. And, in the case of some of us, eating has led us to other passions that have helped us to thrive.

Unfinished

Kira Donnell

I grieve you in little pieces
that grow back much too quickly.
Are you the reason
or simply the excuse?
I will never speak your name
but it is always there
ready to leap forth from my lips,
familiar
like a stone worn smooth.

I find you in ways I can
try to understand,
learn who you are
through nominalized verbs and
late-night history channel specials.
But the hollowness within
is far more vast
than continents and native tongues.
I define myself through your absence
clumsily filling in blanks
wondering which parts you started
that I attempt to finish.

Epistolary

Kira Donnell

Sunset at the beach,
the dog chases seafoam
back and forth
along the shore,
eyes bright with the sheer joy
of feeling that wet fine sand
grit beneath her nails.

I am composing letters to you
as I walk,
each footprint
a word
bearing the weight
of who I am.

High tide
and the waves will gather
all my thoughts
and words
and dance steps
and carry them to you,
waiting on the other side,
on the coast where I was born
in the Land of the Morning Calm.

To Be Adopted: To Be Chosen

Kimberly Faunce

Dear Holt International:

I am writing to you because I was inspired by the article in the Fall 2008 *Hi Families* magazine written by Alice Evans, "I Was Hungry and You Gave Me Food." My name is Kimberly Faunce, and I was adopted from Korea through Holt in 1968. At the time of my adoption, I was six months old and weighed not much more than one pound per month of my age. My understanding of what happened to me was that I was abandoned at birth, brought to City Hospital, and put into foster care. While in foster care, the formula provided for me was probably divided amongst all the children in the family. Do not get me wrong, I do not for a moment fault the foster mother. As a mother of three, I absolutely understand the extraordinarily difficult situation she was in, and I believe that I would have made the same decision. My parents were notified that they should pick a different child because it was unlikely that I would survive, and if I did survive, I would likely be severely mentally retarded.

It is absolutely true that "food is part of loving" as Ms. Evans quoted in her article, but it is equally true that love is food. When I was eventually hospitalized with pneumonia and malnutrition, a wise nurse explained to a priest, Fr. Lucien

Mulhern, that I was starved for love and the physical touch that a baby would normally receive from her parents. The two of them took turns holding me as often as they could. In addition, the Sisters of the Sacred Heart and their students in Seoul sent someone each day to hold me and play with me for the 3–4 months I was hospitalized (my mother was teaching at their sister school in Tokyo at the time). Miraculously, much to the bewilderment of the doctors, I steadily began to improve. Finally, in February 1968, I was deemed healthy enough to go home with my parents.

Five and a half years ago, my family was blessed with the newest addition to our family, our son Michael (aka Kim Dong Yeob), also adopted from Korea. I have to admit that adopting Michael really felt like bringing things full circle. He has been and continues to be a true joy in our lives. His sisters adore him, and he adores them. Looking into the future, I am hopeful that the coincidental fact that we live in a very diverse geographic area with a large Asian population will help him never feel the "outsider syndrome" that I think many adoptees feel during their childhood, myself included.

While my personal experience has been extremely positive, I have heard about and/or witnessed cases that did not work out as well as mine. In 1999 my husband and I attended the First International Gathering of Korean Adoptees sponsored by Holt International in Washington, D.C. There were many adoptees who passionately relayed very negative adoption experiences. I distinctly remember the case of a woman who spoke of constantly being discriminated against by her adoptive parents because she was adopted (unlike the other children). What a horrible situation! So unlike my experience growing up where the mindset was more like "to be adopted means to be chosen."

Sincerely,
Kimberly N. Faunce (aka Kim Yong Hee)

My Lost Chapters

Cheryl S. Hagen

My parents, three sisters, and one brother remember the day I arrived in Honolulu, Hawaii, as if it happened yesterday. Initially, they had asked for a boy; and even after learning I was a girl, they proceeded with my adoption as planned because they already loved me as their own. During the car ride home, I tried to wipe the dirt off my sister's face but, the dirt would not come off because they were in actual fact, freckles! At the age of eighteen months, I began my new life as Cheryl Sun Wha Joy, with "Sun Wha" being the only part of Korea to remain with me.

Being raised in an LDS family, I learned that families can live together forever and often found myself thinking about my birth family and wondering if I'd ever be reunited with them again. I'd try to imagine why they chose to give me away and how difficult it must have been to make that decision. I never felt resentment but still held these questions throughout my life.

When we left the more diverse state of Hawaii for Utah and then Michigan, it started to become difficult. I was teased about looking different. I never really fit in with the other children, and I felt like I was in a maze trying to find the right path to feeling complete.

As a young lady, I chose to get married instead of serving an LDS mission. My husband of the same faith is Norwegian, and we live in Norway with our son and two daughters. Being a stay-at-home mother was always my first priority; and as I watched my children blossom, I kept wondering if they shared similarities with my birth family. After my mother passed away, I thought about them even more, especially my birth mother, and wanted to begin my search. I wanted to learn my heritage so I could pass it down to my children. I did not know how to begin and it seemed hopeless because I had no information regarding my adoption.

While browsing for information regarding birth family search on the Internet, I found a web site where forty Korean adoptees would be selected to travel to their "motherland" for the first time, and birth family search would be the main focus. I would be able to experience Seoul with forty other Korean adoptees from all over the world—adoptees who share similar lives and thoughts as myself. After pondering the idea for few days, I decided to apply and ended up being one of the forty participants selected for the trip. My eyes filled with tears of joy because my lifetime wish was about to come true. Perhaps this would be the chance to learn about my adoption and maybe reunite with my birth family.

At the Oslo airport it was hard to leave my family behind, but I had their support. On the flight to Seoul I still couldn't believe what was happening and I kept pinching myself to make sure I wasn't dreaming.

On the morning of my birthday, the other adoptees gathered for our meeting and sang Happy Birthday to me. Later that day, we had the opportunity to visit the orphanage where we stayed before being adopted and had the chance to review our adoption files. My agency was Eastern Social Welfare Society and to my surprise they had a birthday cake and also sang Happy Birthday to me. I was speechless both times, but deep down I had a feeling that it wasn't my actual birth date even though the records indicated that it was correct.

We also worked with the Korean media to get our stories out to the public. The night before the live program was to be broadcast, I knelt down in humble prayer to ask God to help me find my family by having them watch the program. My prayer was heard.

For the twenty seconds I was featured on a live KBS television program, my birth father recognized me. However, because his story conflicted with mine, I was not informed until after I returned home. I wasn't home for 24 hours and still jetlagged when I received a phone call from KBS informing me about my birth father. I also received an email from ESWS that confirmed the same news. With the excitement of my trip still fresh, I never had the chance to let it all sink in when more mixed emotions flooded over me.

Since it was the holiday season, I considered this to be the best Christmas present ever—just to know that a part of me was alive and missing me in Korea. The three week waiting period until our DNA results were confirmed seemed like an eternity as thoughts and questions kept entering my mind and I was getting anxious.

Our reunion took place via webcam between Seoul and my home in Norway. I met my birth father, aunt, and cousins.

My father cried intensely and kept saying in Korean that he was sorry and regretted letting me go. Tears flowed down my cheeks, and I wished I could give him a hug. My cousin pointed out that I was quiet just like my father. During our phone meeting most of the questions I had were answered. But I still wondered about my birth mother and why my father didn't wish to share information that could lead me to finding her.

My birth mother left my father and divorced him soon after I was born. The divorce tore him apart, and he turned to alcohol for comfort. At the time, he was living with my grandmother, and it was she who took care of me because my father was not well enough to care for an infant. When I was eleven months old, my grandmother did what she thought was best for me and took me to the nearest orphanage with only my name and birth date on a piece of paper. Later, she regretted this and tried to find me, but she didn't have any luck and was told I had already been adopted. I was actually placed at another orphanage and was under the care of my foster mother. It was my grandmother's wish to find me before she passed away—but that did not happen and she died a few years ago.

I learned from my birth father that my Korean name is really Sun Han and my birth date is ten days earlier than my records indicated. I was filled with even more mixed emotions as I wondered what my grandmother's intentions were and why my father never gave a straight answer.

My naturalization papers, marriage certificate, and passport, among other official documents, now contained incorrect information about me. My American family knows me as Sun Wha, but to my Korean family I am Sun Han. The same differences applied with my birth date, and I was confused about which day to celebrate. I felt caught in the middle but decided to leave things as they have been. After all, changing a document doesn't change who I am on the inside.

I arranged to spend some time with my Korean family and went there alone while my husband and children stayed behind once again. A translator was there to meet me at the airport along with my birth father. My father was in tears just as he was during our webcam reunion, and he held my hand as we sat in the back seat of the translator's car. We had our first meal together, and later my cousin joined us and we took a two hour bus ride to my aunt's home. At that time, we had no translator and with the language barrier, it was a challenge communicating even simple thoughts with each other.

To my surprise, my birth mother was located, and I was able to meet her in my birth father's apartment. With a translator present, I was able to ask her some questions. Just before we dropped my mother off at the bus station, we visited the location of where she gave birth to me. The house had been replaced with a paved road, and as the three of us stood there, I noticed that both my mother and father were in tears just as I was.

This second trip to Korea was different from my first one because I was able to experience traditions of living in a Korean home. During my first trip, we stayed in a high class hotel within the big city of Seoul and were individually catered according to our needs.

For the most part, everyone treated me with kindness and I enjoyed spending time with my family. However, the morning I was about leave to stay with my mother, my father turned into a different person, and he tried to prevent me from leaving that day. His temper flared, and he ruined the gifts that I had given him. I was terrified of him and cried during the two hour bus ride thinking he was a harmful man and forgetting all that was pleasant about him. The love and trust we had built during our previous days together suddenly diminished and my last impression of him was "Who is this man?"

When it was just my mother and I together, she showed me pictures of herself when she was younger and I showed her pictures of my family. Later that evening we exchanged gifts, and I met more family members, including my half brother. My cousin translated as my mother told me more of her side of the story.

Shortly after I was born, my mother left my father and filed for a divorce because of his bad temper and alcohol problems. Remembering how I had just parted with him, I could understand this. It was a difficult choice for her because she was also leaving me behind. Back then the fathers automatically gained custody of the child since he was the main provider of the household and the mothers didn't have any rights. When my mother found a secure place to live, she contacted my father to ask how I was doing. My father informed her that I was dead, but deep down she believed I was still alive. My heart almost stopped when I heard this.

My grandmother came and sat next to me and spoke a few words face to face. I did not understand her, but she looked at me, touching my face as I looked at hers. Wondering if we shared the same thoughts, it seemed that I was looking at a mirror image of myself, only older. That night I slept with my mother on her heated marble bed with her hand holding mine until we drifted off to sleep. It was a moment that I wished would last forever.

The next day at the airport I could not help the tears from flowing down my cheeks. After we said our farewells, I remember the last image of my family with smiles. I still keep in touch with my mother and even my father. Even though there were doors opened that weren't expected, I'm happy that I chose to follow this path and to have this chapter in my family history complete.

More Voices

Danielle Koehler

One of the things I believe is that everything happens for a reason. I find myself forcing people to believe that statement. When they don't, you'll hear me going on and on for about thirty minutes explaining why this statement is true. I believe that everything you do in life comes back to you ten-fold.

When I was younger, I never understood the concept of 'color.' I never understood that there was a difference between black, white, Hispanic, Asian, or any other ethnicity. Someone could be purple, pink, or orange, and I really wouldn't have known the difference. We were brought up in a household where the color of your skin DID NOT matter in any way. I remember when I asked my big brother what color I was, and he answered that I was yellow. So whenever anyone asked me what color I was, I would say "yellow." One day my mother heard it come out of my mouth, and I couldn't understand why she was looking at me the way she was.

I grew up in a small town with a population of less than 300 people. A town with no stoplights, a town with a church, a bar, and a post office; a town that looked like a country music video with one of those big whiskery things blowing in the wind. The town next to us was a little bigger and had everything that you really needed. A mall, grocery store, bars, bowling alleys, wonderful lakes; a regular-sized town, but still small enough that when I went to church, it was obvious I was the only Asian girl in that gigantic Catholic church.

I have a big immediate family with my older sisters, Heidi and Robyn, my older brothers, Chris and Josh, and my loving parents, Jim and Ann. I am the baby of the family. Heidi and Chris are white, and Robyn, Josh, and I are all from Korea and Asian. When they say there are different personalities in each individual family, you could pinpoint ours like no other. We have every different variety of people you could ask for.

This is how I describe my family through my eyes. Heidi is the older sister I always looked up to when I was young. We have an eleven-year age gap, but when she is around, you can pretty much bet I am right by her side. If she broke her ankle, I would pretend mine was broken too. If she had her boyfriends over, I would attach to them like they were my own. After ALL those times of annoying her, she always, always was there for me. She never got mad at me, never raised her voice at me, and never got impatient with me. Heidi always is just the big sister that is there for me no matter what.

My older brother Chris is something of an illusion to me. Sadly, I have only a handful of memories of him, and I really can't remember too much about him. He didn't enjoy being around that much, and by age 17 he was out the door and never looked back. The memories I do have of him are all good, and I'm glad that I can look back and think of those.

My brother Josh is the overly protective one and goofball of the family. He will protect me until the day I die, and for that I will forever be grateful. But trust me when I say this— he will also make my life a constant battle of making fun of me!

My sister Robyn is the 'perfect' one. The one that went to school, earned a master's degree, married the man of her dreams, built her gigantic house, had a gorgeous kid, and has never had a late payment in her life. She went through a lot when she was younger but became a beautiful, successful woman. I will always admire her and feel if we lived closer together, we'd be best friends.

I love all my brothers and sisters—for how loveable, annoying and funny they can be. I appreciate them and thank God they are in my life, and I do not take them for granted any second of the day. I know that I'm no walk in the park to get along with, so I appreciate that they love me for who I really am.

I cannot tell my story without mentioning my parents. In my view to be a parent you have to be selfless—to adopt a child, you have to be ready and selfless—especially to adopt five children! My parents are the most loving, kind-hearted, generous, outgoing, funny, gentle, humble, and sane people

I know. They have been married thirty-five years and gone through everything together. They have stuck by each other through the good and bad and still have eyes for each other. They are the definition of true love.

I think being adopted is different in many people's eyes. I remember sitting at a restaurant and two guys asked me if I was an "a.k." I responded that I had no clue what they were talking about. They told me it meant that I was an adopted Korean, and they could tell by the way I walked, dressed, and looked. I'd never felt so stereotyped before. They tried to brush it off as if it was a compliment, but after that day, I often thought about it.

When I moved to Minneapolis, I was 22 years old and it was the biggest culture shock of my life. I had never seen people of so many different races, and I wasn't used to it. People would always invite me to Asian things and tell me what nights were 'Asian' at the clubs and ask me if I knew so-and-so because I was Asian. Walking into an Asian restaurant, they speak to me like I know what they are saying. If an Asian family shops at the store where I work, they bee-line it to me because they think I will be able to understand them. After a couple years living here I have the reputation of being the 'whitest Asian women' ever.

I have always been curious to see where I came from, what my biological parents look like and to know if I have other brothers and sisters. Sometimes I find myself in life predicaments and blame it on the fact that I'm adopted and the way that I was brought up. Then I remember I would not have wanted to be brought up any other way.

I believe it's true that you can really change someone's life. Every passing minute is another chance to turn it all around. We are all meant for great things. We are all meant for happiness. We are all meant for chances. And we are all meant to be here. My parents chose us for a reason, and I wouldn't want it any other way. Then again, everything happens for a reason. ;-)

A Chosen Child

Jennifer Snyder

I grew up in Minnesota in a small community north of the Twin Cities. This community was in the early stages of development and the population was far from diverse. As a result, I grew up in a predominantly Caucasian environment. This really did not create any problems for me as I was not raised to think of myself as being different from anyone else.

I cannot recall a time when I did not know the definition of adoption, or a time when I was not aware that my brother and I had been adopted. This was a topic of discussion in our home as soon as my brother and I were able to understand what it meant. I remember my parents had a book about adoption that was specifically written for children. This book described adopted children as chosen children. This description meant a lot to me, and I've always kept that with me.

I was definitely raised to know where I came from and to be proud of it; however I was never labeled or defined by the fact that I was Korean. Growing up, people were often surprised when my brother and I would introduce ourselves as brother and sister. These reactions never caused us any confusion or made us feel uncomfortable because we were not raised to think this was unusual. This was our family. Period.

I never felt as if my parents built parameters around me or treated me any differently because of where I came from.

Just like all children, I was allowed to be a child and grow into the person I chose to be. My life did not revolve around being an adopted Korean child nor was it a primary focus of my upbringing. I thank my parents for that freedom.

I grew up in a neighborhood with many children, mostly boys. At the time, the only difference I noticed between the other children and myself was that I was the only girl. As I got older and started school, this gradually began to change. The other children were all of a sudden very aware that I did not look like everyone else and these differences were constantly scrutinized, magnified, and verbalized. Quite often I was teased for having black hair, dark skin, and slanted eyes, which would send me home in tears. My brother was very protective and did his best to defend and shield me from this. My parents would soften these blows by reassuring me of how special I was. I was very fortunate to grow up with an abundance of ongoing acceptance, love, and support.

Many things have changed since I was adopted. I think adoption agencies now place more emphasis on maintaining a sense of cultural awareness for internationally adopted children. Adoptive parents will travel overseas to meet their child and bring them home. The circumstances surrounding my adoption were completely different. My parents have never been to Korea. I was not involved in any Korean cultural awareness activities, nor did I ever take part in any support groups for adopted children. I didn't try Korean food until I was in my mid-twenties. I have yet to return to Korea, but I hope to do that very soon.

Being adopted has obviously affected my life in many ways. How could it not have? For me, I view the experience as being positive. It's part of my path in life which has ultimately shaped who I am today. This experience, along with the manner in which my parents raised me, has provided me with many important life lessons that I still carry with me today. I have learned not only to accept differences in others, but also to celebrate them. I have learned the importance of being confident and secure within your own self. I have learned that strength and determination will pull me through even the most difficult of times. I have learned how to love and how to let others love me. I have learned admiration for my parents who adopted two children and raised them to understand what their backgrounds were and also provided them with the freedom to write their own futures. These are just a few of the life lessons I rely on, believe in, and draw from daily.

Some people view adoption as one of those sensitive and uncomfortable topics that should be steered clear of during conversation. Perhaps it should be grouped right along with politics and religion. Honestly I have never been able to figure out why it is looked upon in this manner. When parents adopt a child, they are making a conscious decision to become parents. Why is that a bad thing? I have actually had people tell me they were sorry to hear that I am adopted or give me a look that says, "Oh, you poor thing." Others have asked me if I will ever try to locate my "real parents." I always respond by telling them that I already know my real parents. They are the parents who have been there for me every day of my life.

When I think of adoption, not one negative thought enters my mind. Being adopted did not present me with a handicap or an obstacle to overcome. It never caused me to be ashamed, embarrassed, or even offended when people ask me about it. Instead, I am very proud to be an adopted child and would welcome the opportunity to share my experience with anyone.

Among the greatest life lessons I have learned is having a sense of self. To me, this means really knowing yourself, not only who you are and where you come from, but also your desires, your capabilities, and your limitations. Many people have told me that they consider me to be "a well adjusted individual." They tell me that they find this rather amazing since I know virtually nothing about the birth parents or the country I was born in. They are surprised that I did not encounter any significant problems from being raised by Caucasian parents in a mostly white community. They say this would have caused them uncertainty or confusion about who they are or where they belong. I can honestly say that I have never experienced this because I know exactly who I am. I am a chosen child who came here because my parents wanted a child to love.

Blank Memory

Susan Tiedemann

Brittle corpses fall from the trees,
entombing the burnt flesh of the earth
where hay-colored blemishes of parched grass
mar fields of green.
Autumn quickens the slow pulse of sweltering summer,
yet foreshadows the desolate chill of winter.

A little girl has a blank memory
lurking in the recesses of her unconscious.
Shattered fragments and tender echoes
flutter just beyond her grasp,
inciting vestiges of anguish to pierce the periphery.

Abandoned outside the First Bank of Taejon,
no birthdate, no name,
she looks about one.
Do you think her Uma looked back when she walked away?
Looked back to a tear-streaked face
and heard cries that ring in her ears to this day?

Perhaps this day finds her birth mother long gone,
her flame as fleeting as the memory she left behind.
Were you too poor?
Still a child?
Did he love you?
Or were you also abandoned?

Midas-touched leaves drift to the ground,
auburn and amber
marmalade and ochre,
taking their last flight in the autumn air.

I have a blank memory,
not in my mind but in my heart.
It holds your face and the year we spent together,
boarded up nooks and crannies in my soul
where spiders silently weave their glistening patterns of
beaded strands.

I want to remember the fall of '82,
when you gave me the gift of another chance.
I wonder how you are, and I want to tell you that I am okay.
I have a blank memory waiting for your breath of life.

Bare trees just rustle in the wind.

Fragile Hope

Karen Lairamore Petty

Shadows overcast my heart
as I wander through the streets.

Amidst the puddles of dark despair
are little toes and muddy feet.

Around the bend, I long to see
the familiar face I dream about.

But time wears down my tiny smile
and my little dress fades paper thin.

Fragile hope of a mother's love
overwhelms my soul untouched.

Looking up at the cloudy sky
pours down heavy needle drops.

Leaving tracks across my face
from the dirt washed away.

Prickly wet from the storm
I run to find a place to hide.

In that moment of escape
I feel a tug from behind.

That pulls me tenderly
back where I belong.

Swiftly turning I'm surprised
to see the face I dream about.

Double Identity

Karen Lairamore Petty

I am the girl you want
but I live for someone else

I am the name you know
but my name is one forgotten

I am the face you see
but I know not the reflection

I am the hands you hold
but the lines carry another touch

I am the voice you hear
but the words I speak are foreign

I am a quiet still soul
but the evidence comes from war

I am one mind, one heart, one hope
but my spirit has two lives

So I walk across borders unknown
Seeking for my double identity

Short Poems ~ Adoption

Peter Vinyard

1. A little boy ran up to me, he had something to show me. His mom, his dad, and the rest of his family. But as I looked around, all I found, was a young man standing in front of me. When he told me his name, I thought "we look the same" but when I looked in the mirror, he disappeared, saying he was my apparition.

2. I always try, but sometimes I cry .. about this hand, that I was dealt .. but then I, think that my .. mind will prevent, a life of hell .. so when I, sit and sigh .. I know that things, will go well .. I can't deny, that as I try, with all my might, things won't be right .. but I will tell, my past "fare well" .. as I sit and try .. to deny......

3. I just want to be free, from all that binds me. I just want to see, all that's hidden from me. I just want to be, to some degree, free from being an adoptee. I just want to be, allowed to be me.

4. Wishing that the snow would fall, I hear my homeland start to call, I need to know my history, so I can keep my sanity, but the man, keeps it in the can, just because I'm an Adoptee ..

5. Opened my eyes to realize, I lost sight of the real life, stuck in the past, not lookin' ahead, not feelin' alive, not feelin' dead, not feelin' free, I feel like a zombie.

6. Is pondering days past, knowing they wouldn't last, I lived them all, till I ran outta gas, now I'm runnin' on fumes, everything's a haze, but what can I do, about yesterday, so I fill up the tank and start to sing, about whatever ~ tomorrow may bring.

7. The past is the past, time does not last, so we try to look ahead, stuck in the past instead. We keep trying to progress, with everything no less. But time is not my friend, to the bitter end. All I wanted was time, even spent my last dime, to try and make it mine, but it ripped out my spine, that's where I drew the line, asked the one divine. Will I ever be free? He answered, not until the day, you meet me.

8. As I sit and ponder why .. Thoughts start to sigh .. Life begins to dry .. So I try
I try with all of my might .. Hold on to dreams tight .. Put on the biggest fight .. So I try
Then I cry inside .. Nothing left to hide .. Emotions already dried .. So I try
Pain can be healed .. Mended and sealed .. Go another round .. Was I found ?
I tried ....

Adoption Reunion—
A Search for Connection

Nancy McCullough

In 2010, I was among 25–30 adult adoptees who returned to Hong Kong for an adoption reunion. Most adoptees were from New Zealand, the United Kingdom, and the United States, with a few from other countries. For most of us, this was the first time we returned to our birth country with the intention of meeting other adoptees. This was my intention, along with reconnecting with my place of birth.

It was very emotional. Most of us had not met before, but there was an immediate bonding that occurred as we shared our experiences. Some of us were from the same orphanage, during the same time. We could have been play mates or even crib mates. I was three and a half years old when I was adopted. I have no memory of the orphanage or ever living in Hong Kong, and yet I felt a close connection to many of the attendees. I felt like I was attending a family reunion and meeting with long lost relatives.

I am from the Fanling Babies Home, and while I was in Hong Kong, a group of us who from this orphanage visited the site where it used to stand. Although it was torn down years ago, as we all stood on the sidewalk of that special place of our beginnings—we were home. Although what is there now has no resemblance to the previous orphanage, there was some strange feeling of familiarity. For me this feeling intensified when we walked across the street to a dilapidated market. Our caretakers shopped at this market, so for me this was the real connection to my past. Most people looking at this market would think it was an ugly sore spot that should be torn down. Yet to me there was something wonderfully attractive about it. I found myself imagining what it would have looked like 50 years ago and pictured myself eating food from this market. I yearned for a taste from my past.

To my knowledge, everyone was adopted into Caucasian families except for me. Both of my adoptive parents are Canadian-born Chinese. During the '50s and '60s, the years most of us attending the reunion were adopted, social workers told our adoptive parents to "assimilate the children into your culture." In other words, don't worry about their Chinese heritage; get them adapted into their new homes as quickly as possible. They thought children came with a blank slate (no past) and could easily be molded into any family and culture they are placed into. Today, psychologists and social workers know this is not true.

As people shared, there seemed to be recurring themes. Many shared that they didn't fit in with their adoptive families as they didn't resemble their parents. When they did meet up with the Chinese community nearby, they didn't fit in there either because of the language barriers. Some were unfamiliar with the Chinese culture. The theme surfaced about three families, our birth family, our adopted family, and the Chinese adoptee family. They only felt accepted and understood by those in the latter family.

This feeling of not belonging and identity crisis was exacerbated when some of us attempted to obtain our Hong Kong ID card. It was our understanding that in order to possess this ID, we had to be able to show paperwork that proved how our names changed from birth to the present. The immigration officer was going by the letter of the law. He found fault with each person's paperwork. For most who had birth certificates (I was not one of them), there was no last name on the birth certificate. Yet when we were adopted, a last name mysteriously appeared on the adoption certificate. The officer said, "The names are different, so you cannot prove that this person is you!" Another of us showed a document that said, "Copy," and he insisted that we had to have the original.

At some point we realized that even if we had all the correct original paperwork that proved how our names changed from the birth certificate to our current passport—it wasn't enough. The officer looked at one of the birth certificates and said, "There are no birth parents listed." There was a slash under both the mother's and father's name. It clearly stated that this child was abandoned, so how could there be a name for the father or mother? I kiddingly said, "They didn't leave a note." He was not amused and said that without a mother or father's name, the authorities cannot verify that our parents were "Chinese." I felt like saying, "Have you looked at us? Don't we look Chinese?" One stated that she knew people who were abandoned, who had no birth parents listed, and yet they were able to get their Hong Kong ID. In fact, we knew that one of the adoptees attending the reunion obtained their Hong Kong ID. It didn't matter what anyone said as it was obvious that this officer wasn't budging. I was totally frustrated and felt like I was spinning my wheels with no way out. I was getting a headache over this so I walked away to spend my time with a couple of my new family members.

Not everyone trying to obtain their ID card had a strong desire to live or work in Hong Kong at the present time. So at first I didn't understand why this was so important to the others. Then it finally sank in. They wanted to feel like they were accepted and could belong. They had been rejected by their birth mother, and felt like a "misfit" in both their adopted families and the Chinese community in their area. Now they are being rejected by their mother country. My heart aches for them and pray that they will be able to get their Hong Kong IDs in spite of the obstacles. I also pray that this will help bring closure and a sense of peace, giving them a sense of acceptance.

For me, my sense of belonging and peace comes from my faith and my relationship with Jesus Christ. I shared with the group that there are actually four families. The first three have been discussed, but there's a fourth family and that's God's family. This is a family that we can all belong to, and be adopted by our Heavenly Father who loves and accepts us unconditionally. In our lives, we had no choice in our birth or adopted families, but we can choose to belong to God's family. This is the one family we can all fit into and find our home and identity.

I understand the deep void that many people expressed as I too felt that earlier in my life. I was in my late thirties when I went through the experience of reliving my abandonment.

It came on totally unexpectedly. All of a sudden I felt a deep pain within me. I started to cry. It's hard to describe; all I know is it felt like an incredibly deep and intense hollow feeling. It was a wrenching pain I had never experienced before. All I could do was cry. I had no idea where the pain was coming from and no idea what it was.

Week after week, I would feel this intense pain. As time passed, an image was added. There was a little child crying as loudly as she could, flailing her arms and legs in a rocking-type motion from side to side. After seeing this same image a few more times, I realized the child was me. I had no idea how old I was or where I was. All I knew was there was a darkness that seemed to go forever. My ailment didn't get any better. In fact, it got worse. Finally, after weeks of agony, I had a good friend suggest I seek professional counseling. After weeks of sessions, she was able to interpret the image I kept having. It was me when I was abandoned.

Why did I need to experience the abandonment issue again? My analytical mind thought, "Surely once is enough!" Since I was only a few days old when I was abandoned, I assumed I was way too young to remember the traumatic event. The image I had engrained in my mind never concluded with someone finding me and taking me to an orphanage. I was just in turmoil the whole time. I wanted to heal and move on. I couldn't see how reliving the story over and over again was beneficial.

I asked the Lord what He wanted me to learn from these heartfelt recurring feelings and emotions. In time, I came to realize that I had never grieved the loss of my birth parents, and I needed to. I felt God telling me I needed to first acknowledge the pain and then embrace it instead of trying to run away from it. I could somehow acknowledge the pain but embracing it was another story. This pain was buried so deep that for over thirty years I never let it surface.

During one counseling session, I relived the pain right in front of her. She encouraged me to let go of the pain and release it to the Lord rather than to try and clamp down and fight it. At first, I was afraid because I didn't know what would happen. I feared the experience would become so overwhelming I would break. Yet something inside said, "Okay Lord, I trust you enough to get me through this." Immediately, the pain intensified to another level and I began to wonder if my fears were true. Then all of a sudden, it burst like a balloon that popped. The release came, and I knew God had healed me. My abdominal muscles were still aching, but the intense, unbearable pain was gone.

The complete healing came a couple of years later. God brought me back to the image of when I was flailing my arms and legs. This time, the pain wasn't nearly as bad. Then all of a sudden, in my mind's eye, I saw the hand of God pick me up and cradle me. He then handed me to my adoptive parents. Finally, He gave me the answer. At that moment I felt a love within me that far exceeded any love a human being can give. God was impressing upon me the fact He was in control of my life and had been caring for me since my birth to the present time.

The Souls of Clear Folk[1]

Stephen Johnson

How do you see
the souls of those whose bodies are invisible?
To me, to be human
Is to also be indivisible
So when they say there's no shame
That we're all the same,
There's nothing more dismissible.

You see, in my journey to be whole,
I find myself sitting in one
Stuck in a rut, with nothing but
The media, our culture's encyclopedia
Preaching insanity, profanity, inhumanity
A blindspot, in this melting pot
To tell me, to be

Everything that I am not

Let me ask ya'll a question
When you look at me
What's your first impression?
Does the sight of me
Leave you guessin'
Or am I just that kid who presented
At one of those breakout sessions

Do I look like someone
Who wants to be freed from oppression?
Depression, suppression

Let me teach you a lesson
Can you hear what I'm stressin'?

So, tell me, what color are the souls born in Seoul?
Who grew up with holes
Because nobody knows
What it's like
To be froze...
Frozen between lives
The lives between times
What time? I'm stuck in this rhyme
To be two things at one time
And *nothing*
At the same time

When neither side accepts me
as one of their own
I feel at home when I'm alone
Or when everyone else
Is down off their thrones
Joining me down in this danger zone

That's when I feel known

But I'm here
To be in this fight
Not just to be right
But so we can take flight
Because to be adopted means
To have light in the night
Am I right?

The metaphor that says that we're all better
For avoiding the war and the gore
Settling scores, selling babies like some corner store

But must you ignore my internal war?

The one that keeps me up at night.
Wondering where my mother lies.
Does my father's memory still have ties to mine?

I grew up hating kimchi
A white-washed wannabe
Can't you see me?
Or am I invisible, imperceptible, undetectable
At times *intellectual*
You choose to see me like Hollywood
In some movie scene
Lookin' like Mr. Bean
Fixin' a computer screen
Or solvin' the square root of eighteen
(BTW, it's 3 times the square root of 2)

So, don't act like you know me
Unless you can show me
What it's like to fall.
To sit here and be with me
When, in the end, that's all anyone could ask for.

You see, I used to be in awe
Think I had some fatal flaw
Up against the wall
Or exist in some impossible natural law
Thank you and
Kamsahamnida

Because I am now free
Free to be the whole me
I *love* Kimchi
Hanboks, Bimbimbap
Banchon, Busan, Ee Taw Wan

I don't wanna hide
Hasn't been a fun ride
Ask those with whom I confide
But I also like that apple pie
Good 'ol American French fries
I can even be
That Texas tough guy
But I don't know why
In the blink of an eye
Someone has to hate me
Call me a chinky eyed wannabe

Look at my eyes
I'm not surprised
I've got nothing to hide
I'm the one with the prize.

And I will rise.
In the midst of the flies and the lies
And the look in their eyes
And in the end, we will rise.

We will rise.

We will rise past the times.
And the grimes and the crimes
against our humanity.
Man, if I had a dime for every time
Some kid decided to chime in with
A joke that felt more like
falling off a bike or goin' on a hunger strike

Again, we will rise.

Against all the tides.
And the size of our seemingly insurmountable disguise
We will rise.

Because behind all the lies,
There's ten more good guys (and gals)
Our pals here at KAAN and KAAP and IKAA
and GOA'L and HOLT and ASK
And don't forget about Also Known As.
Because we should all be known as
Together

Those who rise.

So, before we go and break out the soju
Munchin' on our mandoo
Let me ask of you
Just one more task of you
That this won't be the last
Time that you listen
That you won't start dismissin' or reminiscin'
Every time someone tells you their story
Just listen.

You see, because the thing here
Is that we've all got pain near
And it's been that way forever.
And we need each other now
More. Than. Ever.

---

1 The title from this was inspired by W. E. B. DuBois's essay titled *The Souls of Black Folk*, published in 1902. DuBois describes the feelings of "otherness" felt by African Americans in the United States. He describes this as "double consciousness," living their lives "through the eyes of others." The adoptee story is similar to what some have called "triple consciousness"—not feeling fully Korean, or entirely the ethnicity of our adoptive families, but existing rather in some third space. Much of this poem was also inspired by the writings of Maya Angelou, particularly her famous work, titled *Still I Rise*. Much credit must also be given to all those who have courageously walked before me, blazing a trail for me to a voice.

The Yin Yang: Dialectical Symbolism

Kelsay Myers

❧

As a child, I was prone to collecting things: *Skybox* baseball and basketball cards, pencils, and pogs. Coming home from school, I'd beg to go to *Rookies*, the local comic book and card-collectors store, where at that time, they knew me by name. I was the only girl there, and I stood out in my black patent leather shoes and pigtails buying holograms of Michael Jordan and Scottie Pippen, the occasional *Mighty Morphin Power Rangers* comic, and a lot of pogs with pictures of poisonous roses, laughing skulls, and ticking time bombs on their faces. One afternoon I came across a yin yang while carefully poking through the boxes at the front of the store. Intent on finding exactly the right pog, I made sure to look at each one individually in order not to miss a single detail. When I saw the yin yang for the first time, I was immediately attracted to the aesthetics. I knew what I held in my hand had a special meaning, even though I didn't know what it was or where it came from. I would never play that pog on the playground because playing it included the risk of losing it.

❧

I became interested in learning about Korean culture as a child as well. I went to a Korean Adoptee Culture Camp in West Michigan one summer where we cut out pictures of Korean landscapes and cities, made *mandu*, and played with Korean dolls and flags. From the first moment I saw it, I loved that flag, despite pledging my allegiance to a different one. I was immediately attracted to the aesthetics—white, with four different black line patterns in each corner and a red and blue yin yang in the middle.

I remember staring at the book, tracing over the lines with my eyes, then my finger. It's a compulsive habit. My mother says that she can tell when I really love a book because I stare at it, run my fingers over the pages, and smell it. I do it unconsciously, but it must involve the desire to get closer to whatever image or thought is inside the book. I read that on the flag, the yin yang represents harmony in opposition, and the lines denote heaven and earth, east and west. I was just a child when I tried to touch South Korea through its flag.

Which came first—the pog or the flag? I really don't remember anymore. It's like dialectical symbolism. Which came first—being Korean or being American? Faulty memory aside, my mind is attracted to the aesthetics of dualism. I'm reminded of the dialectic every time I'm asked, "Are you Korean?" and I pause before saying, "Yeah, I'm Korean."

I was born in Pusan, South Korea, and I know next to nothing about it. I spent the first three months of my life there in foster care waiting to fly to America. I love the flag. The main religions are Buddhism and Christianity. The martial arts form is *tae kwon do*. The capital is Seoul. I know that I'm supposed to like *kimchee* and that *sarang* means love. *Kong* is river. I spell *bul go ki* wrong, but I know the difference between a peasant and a queen's *hanbok*. I've been told that I have the "facial features" of Pusan. I know that Pusan is really *Busan*. My Korean name is *Jin Jung Mee*, and I do know how to pronounce it, though it took 24 years for me to figure it out. I own some traditional rainbow rubber shoes, a shirt that says "Bare" with a picture of a bear underneath it, a marble tea set, and a passport that expired over two decades ago. Yeah, I'm Korean.

A professor once asked me to "define dialectics," but it wasn't a standard definition he was after. He wanted to know what it meant to *me*. Despite my training in philosophy, I didn't understand dialectics personally. I couldn't think of a response more complex than it being about two opposites in dialogue with each other through a kind of paradoxical process—*the yin* and *the yang*. He didn't disagree but said that was only one way of looking at it. He had been taught to think about dialectics as the development of a rose. You plant the seed, a bud grows, and several factors go into it before it is able to blossom. It's "a process of becoming," like the space between Asian and American—whether it's erased, clearly written, forgotten, or never known.

In *Art as Experience*, John Dewey writes:

> Flowers can be enjoyed without knowing about the interactions of soil, air, moisture, and seeds of which

they are the result. But they cannot be understood without taking just these interactions into account— and theory is a matter of understanding. Theory is concerned with discovering the nature of the production of works of art and of their enjoyment in perception. (11)

Theory *is* a matter of understanding. Theory is about discovering the nature of the production of the self and of its perception in reality.

☯

I became a U.S. citizen when I was 16 because my mother wanted it to be my choice. Unlike other adoptive parents she knew who had their children become citizens upon arrival, she wanted me to be old enough to remember it. I don't. I don't remember the official's face or what he said. I don't even remember what I wore. There wasn't much to remember. I signed my name at the bottom of a piece of paper at the border between Michigan and Canada, and then I was a citizen.

I do remember the looks the other 9th graders shot each other in Civics class when I announced that I could never be president because I wasn't born in America. The mood of the classroom shifted. I went from being one of them to being an outsider. I remember coming home from school that afternoon and telling my mother that I wanted to become a U.S. citizen. And, I remember my parents inviting some of my friends to a surprise party for me after we came back from Canada. They gave me an American flag and a Precious Moments Statue of Liberty while we all ate *kal bi* at Seoul Garden—the aesthetics of an Asian American girl.

☯

Choosing a title is hard. It's not just the aesthetics of it but the dialectics. Some people hate "Dialectical Symbolism" because it's "too complex" and "unnecessary." "The Yin Yang" seems right albeit obvious. I like them both, but I leaned toward "Dialectical Symbolism" if forced to make a choice, everyone else toward "The Yin Yang." The problem with symbolism can be in how significant the signifiers become and how people do (or do not) read them. Is it just me who reads "Dialectical Symbolism" as American (or Western) and "The Yin Yang" as Asian (or Eastern)?

The first time I learned about dialectics was in an Existentialism and Film class my first year of college when we read Søren Kierkegaard's *Fear and Trembling*. His highest form of existence is to become like Abraham, "a knight of faith." Abraham is a "knight of faith" because his passion for his son, Isaac, is so strong that he makes a double movement—a dialectical movement. Abraham loves Isaac and wants to be with him most in the world, so God requires that Abraham sacrifice his son to prove his love for the Lord. Abraham believes so strongly in the Lord that he raises the knife above his head to sacrifice his son, and by his faith alone, the paradoxical occurs, and he gets Isaac back. A "knight of faith," by definition, is dialectical because he or she believes irrevocably in two seemingly contradictory things—the desire *for* (a son) and the decision to kill it (him).

My grandpa would sit and do a jigsaw puzzle to pass time at the lake. It's become a compulsive habit for me. If I start a puzzle, I can't abandon it until all its pieces fit together. Sometimes I think I'm trying to do the same thing with my writing, but the pieces are harder to fit together.

For years, a sword hung above the South Korean flag in my bedroom. I'm still not quite sure what it all meant. The problem is probably me, and my adversity to the natural. A jigsaw puzzle isn't an organic metaphor, neither is a flag or a sword. Flowers are. I could benefit from less meta-levels and more flowers. John Dewey is an example to aspire to. He says:

> Time as organization in change is growth, and growth signifies that a varied series of change enters upon intervals of pause and rest; of completions that become the initial points of new processes of development. Like the soil, mind is fertilized while it lies fallow, until a new burst of bloom ensues. (Dewey, John. *Art as Experience.* New York: Perigee Penguin Group, 1934.)

It is a process of becoming.

The first time I learned about dialectics, I wasn't quite sure what it all meant either. I'm pretty certain, however, that I didn't find Abraham to be an example to aspire to. Yet, if the pieces fit, it must be part of the larger picture. I, too, as a Korean adoptee have the knife hanging above my bed. Like a Kierkegaardian "knight of faith," it is an existence that cannot be fully understood without making a double movement—a dialectical movement. For on the one hand, the adoptee knows that she is American in every way that counts while in the same instance believes it is an adopted identity, for an adopted person, in an adopted country. It is a paradox of authenticity. A transnational adoptee, by definition, is dialectical because he or she holds two seemingly conflicting cultures and identities together inside of her *being*. The desire is to *become* whole while not killing part of oneself in the process.

Friedrich Nietzsche said in *The Gay Science*:

With regard to all aesthetic values, I now make use of this main distinction: I ask in every individual case, "Is it hunger or overflow that has become creative here?" Another distinction would seem to recommend itself more to begin with—it is more obvious by far—namely, paying attention to whether the longing for fixation, eternalization, *being*, is the cause of the creation, or whether it is the longing for destruction, change, the new, the future, *becoming*. (Guignon, Charles and Derk Pereboom, eds. *Existentialism: Basic Writings*. 2nd ed. Indianapolis: Hackett Publishing Company, 2001.)

Maybe growing up means putting away toys like my pog collection, flags, and swords. Tucking them away with paper lanterns, porcelain dolls, my mother's old box of toys and jewelry, my wooden box with the three shell casings from my grandfather's funeral, and the memories. I've replaced my weapons with golden metallic roses that once belonged to my grandmother. Even my flowers are not organic. But, in regard to all aesthetic values, I wonder in every individual case, what is the desire *for* and when is the decision *to*?

Korea 2010

Betsy Schaffer

Entering my eyes
are faces. Their blood
is my blood.
I see temples
and office buildings
blurring into the gray Han
sky. I see BMWs
parked next to kimchi pots.
I need to touch my stomach
to calm the disbelief
that this is where I was born.
I need to stretch my eyes wide
to see why I need to be here
to feel whole.

Though a Child's Eyes

Kevin Riutzel

I was brought over to the States on December 24, 1984. My parents still have a tiny blue replica of the plane. I was brought over on a blanket of misunderstanding.

I've spoken with many adoptees from Korea and there is no one perspective on adoption from us. There is no right or wrong. Some have thrown water cups at restaurants upon the mention of their birth mother, screaming, "I never want to meet her ever!" Some journey back to Korea with the intent of staying in Korea, their country of origin, forever. Some, like me, are just happy that a decision was made to keep life going.

I was brought into a picturesque family in the States—in a suburb of LA with a cottage-like house, a father, a mother, a sister, a brother (me), a dog, a cat, and goldfish. We had a big backyard with a giant persimmon tree in the center and a plum tree on the side. Adjacent to the house was a back patio with a BBQ grill for long summer nights. Most of the neighborhood was Caucasian, however with a Korean family across the street, exposure to one's roots wasn't that far away.

We went to church on Sundays and of course were the only family with faces not quite like the other parishioners. However, the church seemingly understood that we were just another group of people amidst this Lutheran family of families. I went to chorus there, went through confirmation there, and spent most of my holidays there. Our church had this grand entrance with huge double doors leading into the lobby where ushers would hand out programs and greet everyone with warm smiles and hearty hellos.

On a typical Mother's Day, my sister and I woke up early to make Mom sausage, eggs, toast, hash browns, and coffee with a just a dash of cream (too much and she'd say it wasn't really coffee), we went to our church like we would any other holiday. This Sunday, they were handing out pink carnations to all the mothers as they passed by on their way into the sanctuary. Sporting our best Sunday attire, our family walked through the double doors all together, greeted the enthusiastic ushers, received our Mother's Day programs, and then sat down in the left rear area of the sanctuary.

Yet, the ushers never gave my mother a carnation that day. All she received was a smile and a program. They never made the connection that she could be related to the two Asian children walking beside her. She sat down and soon after, welled up with tears and silently cried in the pew.

Situations like this became more common as I grew older and understood the concept of difference more and more. Being greeted by the hostess at a restaurant was never, "Party of four?" but rather, "Party of two?"

We sit at the dinner table at home and everything screams family. Dad turns on Aretha Franklin or Huey Lewis, Mom works busily in the kitchen preparing homemade chili and garlic bread, while my sister and I finish setting the dinner table. We all sit down together with Dad at the head of the table, my Mom and sister one side, and I on the other. We hold hands, say grace, and dig in while talking about the day.

Yet, when we go out for dinner, we must assure the world that we are indeed a good ol' American family. We just look a little different. In the home, life tells us that we are a family; but outside the home, we have to tell life that we are a family.

I normally don't write autobiographical anything. However, it's 4:30 a.m., and I can't go back to sleep still being very jetlagged after my two-and-a-half-week trip to Korea recently. I've already visited Korea two times before this; one visit included a three-month study abroad period at a Korean university, however each visit brings yet another new perspective.

My mother passed away in November 2000 when I was sixteen years old. This means that I have had three mothers look after me as their own and have been separated from each. My birth mother took care of me for nine months, my foster mother for four months, and my mother for sixteen years. Hopefully the time frames support my reluctance in calling my birth mother my 친어머니 ("true mother") as I still do hope to meet her one day.

I now work on the 911 paramedic ambulances for the city I live in due in part from my desire to give back to the field that tried so hard to save my mother from her sudden cardiac arrest in front of a local bookstore while trying to buy me *The Scarlet Letter* for English class. Yet, aside from seeing the end of life on the ambulance and trying to preserve that life as long as possible, on the flip side when you see a newborn baby brought into this world while driving down the road at

40 miles per hour—you cannot help but gain a newfound appreciation for the start of life. This appreciation rings true for my own life, which asked a 23-year-old waitress in a small restaurant in Daegu City to nurture me in her stomach for nine months amidst thoughts of abortion and walls of social stigma, to go through one of the most painful processes in humanity, and then to relinquish me to strangers the day after I was born.

This time when I went to Korea, I officially started my search to find the birth mother. I had looked at my adoption file before, but not with the same exact desire I now have to thank my birth mom. I don't want to go running back to my country of origin and live there forever, nor do I have any anger towards my birth mother for making the difficult choice to give me up for adoption. Instead, I just want to take her out to karaoke, maybe drink some soju (or some other choice non-alcoholic beverage) with her, and tell her how thankful I am for the decisions she's made on behalf of my future.

When we're young, we don't know what a family is. Our mom, dad, or someone older tells you that the group of people sitting down at that table in the mall food court is a family and we just say, "OK." As we get older, we decide what constitutes a family based on what we've learned and what we've experienced. We observe, formulate, and come to a conclusion of our own. One day, I can only hope that we may view families once again through a child's eyes and accept them for what they are—different.

Made in Korea

Chandra Scott

I was so excited about going to Korea.
It's been a while since I've been in this area.
I was there a very long time ago
And now I was flying right into Seoul.

It's what I expected in seeing all the sights:
The tall buildings and the neon's bright lights.
There were familiar names that you'd recognize:
If you guessed McDonald's and Starbucks, you would be
right!

It was interesting to be surrounded by these
People who looked very close to me.
Everyone loved their electronic gizmo,
Even the people that were very old.

The folks there had dark hair and brown eyes.
It made me laugh and smile inside,
Because back in Montana, I was the only one
who even had features of a Korean.

I went with my sister and my niece.
We saw a palace, just us three.
We got a glimpse of royalty long ago.
Of course they're gone; they are no more.

The best part was the food that we ate.
How many bowls did we have? I think over eight!
Kimchi was a staple in this land.
I ate a lot but not with my hand.

We also took a trip to Busan.
It's the place where I came from.
It's so different from the bright lights of Seoul,
Here things were dilapidated, buildings with holes.

It made me appreciate my own country,
Living in America that gave me opportunity.
I know the Almighty was watching over me
And placing me in a home of love and mercy.

So if you decide to travel and go,
Maybe to Ireland or Morocco,
Just remember after you roam,
You have a place that you can call home.

Don't take this wonderful place for granted, please.
You have freedom and choices, not like some countries.
I hope you will stand and proudly say,
"I'm from the land of the U.S. of A."

Now I'd like to end with this necklace I bought.
This three-letter word means a whole lot.
God has given me life with a husband and three boys—
It's summed up in one word and that is "JOY."

The Global Language of Women

Katherine Noel Hyun Ah Sullivan

They were stylishly dressed, had manes of glossy black hair, and could speed walk in stiletto heels. I felt remarkably frumpy clad in khaki shorts, sporting a messy pony tail, and wearing running shoes. The young women in this Pusan hair salon put this New Yorker to shame.

My life had been full the past twenty eight years since I left this city in which I was born. My generous parents had given my four siblings (three of whom were also adopted from Korea) and me the world—steadfast love and encouragement, a childhood on a farm in New Hampshire, music lessons and sports camps, and an excellent education. As a young adult foraying her way into the world, I began a successful career and recently married. But I had never experienced the sights, sounds, tastes, and life of my birthplace.

I arrived in Pusan without much of a plan. I had not initiated a search. I just wanted to experience this place, so I spent my first morning meandering the streets and munching on *pajeon* from a street cart. I noticed groups of beautiful girls my age streaming in and out of one particular storefront so I walked over. Before I knew it, I was sitting in a salon chair pointing to magazine photos with a hairdresser. Our conversation relied on her limited English and my iPod translation app, but somehow we chatted as if we were friends who hadn't seen each other in awhile. She shared with me her favorite stores and bars, and I shared with her my assessment of local hotels and transportation. I was startled when her response to my description of life in America was laced with sympathy— "oh, I've heard it's very dirty and unhealthy there." She explained how her friend had visited New York the year before and described the people as loud, fat, and dowdy. I slumped further in my chair not because she was wrong. In fact, she was correct on many fronts. I slouched because my childhood had been full of the implicit (and sometimes explicit) refrain that life in America was so much better than life in Korea (or any place else for that matter). And she told me it wasn't.

I left the salon thrilled with my haircut but unsettled about our conversation. On one hand, I reminded myself that lots of people are proud of and sometimes defensive of their hometown. How many times had I boasted of New Hampshire's lakes and Norman Rockwell-esque town greens? I was pleasantly surprised that my expectations of Pusan as a weathered port city were largely mistaken and that Pusan actually had a pulse. There are beaches, temples, skyscrapers, consumerism, and art. Pusan was clearly a different city circa 2010 than 1982; however, were the well-intentioned comments, both spoken and unspoken, but always drenched in pity, of how much better my life was in the United States actually wrong? Was she right?

The following day I was determined to buy myself a *hanbok*. The tourist book told me to go to "Street of Hanbok" in Boopyung-Dong so off I went. I am an experienced shopper, but it took me almost ten laps of this area to finally find an obstructed staircase with a single child-size *hanbok* (similar to the one my parents got me at a Holt picnic when I was six years old) hanging from the doorpost to find what I was looking for. The creaky steps reminded me of the underground "shops" of the "real" designer purses sold on Canal Street in New York, but the sight at the top did not. It was floor to ceiling of vibrant silks, tulles, and tafettas. They were magenta, gold, and azure and boasted silver threading and intricate beading. I walked from stall to stall touching the cool fabrics and trying to decide which I liked best.

"*Yeppoyo,*" spoke the older Korean woman that approached me. I furiously dug through my purse to find the iPod translator. Pretty. Did she mean I was pretty or the fabric was pretty? Unclear but presumably the latter, I squeaked out a *kamsahamnida*. Her face immediately lit up, so I quickly followed with *hangukmal mot hae yo* ("I don't speak Korean," compliments once again of the iPod). She nodded. The next hour was spent pointing to the *hanboks* on the walls, touching stunning fabrics, and nodding yes and no. We both spoke the language of shopping.

I finally settled on two *hanboks* that I loved. One was lavender tulle with sprays of silver threading. I imagined wearing it to an event with my strappy sandals and metallic clutch that were buried in my closet on the other side of the world. The other was a sea foam green donned with graceful white flowers. It would be perfect with pearl chandelier earrings. There were now three or four older women measuring, pulling, and tucking my *hanboks* this way and that. One would direct me to stretch out my arms while the other would stand on her tippy toes to ask me to do the same. The pedestal on which I stood was a sight of women, measuring tapes, and scraps of fabric. The experience was quite reminiscent of wedding gown shopping a few years back. Except my mom and sister were not there with me.

My trip to Korea was unfortunately cut short after two days due to a family emergency. But in those two short days I got to know a bit of my birthplace, though not my hometown, my people, or my family.

Pusan and Koreans are in my blood, but New England and Sullivans are in my heart.

Where Do I Begin

Kim Sundell Brown

Most of my curiosity about adoption stems from my life before my first birthday.

There are no pictures of me as a baby. There are no clothes that I may have worn from the hospital.

There are no gifts from someone who would have been happy that I was born. There is nothing from the woman who gave birth to me. Nothing.

Entering the world without fanfare is not bad. Entering the world without fanfare does not make your life meaningless. Entering the world without fanfare is not shameful.

As an adoptee life began precariously. There is a choice to be made whether life continues to be precarious or not. It is a choice!

Metamorphosis:
A Reflection of My Life

Suzanne Swanson

Growing up as an adoptee has been really tough. I knew I was adopted ever since I can remember. My adoptive parents told me that when I came at four months old, I just stared at them for two weeks straight. I was traumatized by the whole event. I have never heard of anyone staring at their adoptive parents for two weeks straight. From there, life has been a roller coaster. It started out when I was young and my parents showing me pictures of me getting off the plane and meeting them. I remember me saying to my mom, "That is sad." My mom didn't know what to do and just shut the photo album.

After the time I reviewed the photo album, I started having problems with being adopted. My identity really didn't become an issue for me until I was in sixth grade. I started struggling with who I was, having feelings of being plucked off the planet that I knew and put on an entirely new one and trying to adapt and survive. I was accepted at my elementary school but when I hit seventh grade, things went downhill. I constantly struggled in school with being bullied, teased, and put down. I also struggled academically, and the teachers were frustrated with me asking lots of questions just to get attention. However, that wasn't true at all. All of this culminated into wanting to commit suicide. I had thought about it every day since ninth grade. The teachers and administration didn't do anything about the bullying; they just acted like it was a normal "phase" people go through in middle school. Those years were horrible.

I graduated from high school and went on to college. I continued to struggle academically but got the help I needed from my teachers. Finally I reached the breaking point, threatened to commit suicide, and was hospitalized. I went to a state psychiatric hospital for one month after being in acute care at my local hospital. That didn't help, but as my psychiatrist said, it kept me alive. When I left the state psychiatric hospital I returned to college.

After struggling for ten years, I finally got the CORRECT diagnosis—multiple Axis I diagnoses and Borderline Personality Disorder on Axis II. I found a doctor that could test me as an adult, and after several meetings I was officially diagnosed with Asperger's Syndrome. It was a relief, but at the same time bittersweet. I was relieved to finally have a diagnosis that fit because since sixth grade I had been treated for major mental illnesses.

Since I was very young I wanted to find my birth mother. I contacted Holt and requested a search. Holt Korea found my birth mother. However, my birth mother was NOT thrilled that I wanted to have contact with her. She told the Holt Korea social worker that she didn't want anything to do with me. I received the news from my post adoption social worker, and my emotions were overwhelming. I wanted to kill myself right there and then. I requested Holt Korea to contact my birth mother for information on my birth father so they could search for him.

This was a risk because my file said my mother was unwed and my father was married. My father had children, and his family would not be happy to learn of me since I was born out of wedlock. This could have potentially destroyed my father's family, but I was desperate to find information about my family. I had longed for information about them since I was young. Holt Korea again contacted my birth mother and told her I wanted information on my birth father. She denied knowing anything about him.

She did tell the social worker I was the oldest child in my family and my mother was married and divorced. I have three sisters and one brother, who at time were ages twenty-two, nineteen, sixteen, and nine. My two oldest sisters (twenty-two and nineteen) knew about me and encouraged my mom to get to know me. The younger siblings did not know of me. My birth mother also told my social worker that she wanted to have contact with me and requested a letter and photos. I was elated with this news and quickly put together a letter and sent photos. I waited and waited for a response. It never came. Holt Korea tried contacting her again, but she changed her phone number so they couldn't find her. I officially gave up hope again and thought that my birth mom didn't want to have anything to do with me. I longed so much for a relationship, but I was being pushed away. I was crushed.

Finally, one day my birth mother walked into the Holt Korea office and brought a letter for me. I got the word that night from my social worker, and he read the letter to me over the phone. I was so excited. I quickly wrote back and asked for photos of her and my siblings.

It has now been about two years, and there has been no response. Once again, I'm crushed. I have officially given up all hope that I will ever have a relationship with my birth mother. I think that she is caught up feeling like she doesn't have a right to be in my life since she gave me up for adoption. However, I told her in my letter that she is my only mother and that nothing will ever change that.

Since it's been at least two years since my first and only letter, I have moved on with my life. But it's tough. It's very tough knowing that your birth mother doesn't want anything to do with you. I am now actively trying to do a sibling search for my two oldest sisters. I am still longing to have that connection to my birth family. I want to go back to Korea and see my country sometime, but at the last minute, I change my mind. Maybe eventually I'll gain enough courage and go back to Korea and see my home country.

Since then, I have found Korean adoptee groups on Facebook to help me with my identity issues. I also found a group in Nebraska for adult Korean adoptees and I have been to a few of the social gatherings. Finding my niche of being with other Korean adoptees experiencing similar identity issues has really helped me.

Looking back at my life, there are areas I definitely wish could have been better. Being adopted was not the best thing that happened to me. Although many people feel fortunate and that their lives are much better being adopted than being in their birth country, I feel the opposite. Despite my feelings I have learned to make the best of it as I continue pursuing my dreams and goals.

Bold Yellow in a Sky of Blue

Loey Werking Wells

My mother likes to say she picked me out of a catalog. Back in the days when mail-order meant thumbing through slick pages crammed with hundreds of pictures, each with a succinct description, I can picture her folding over a corner and setting it aside to show my father later that evening. While I've never seen this catalog, I'm sure that it had a few dog-eared corners. I imagine each page featured a dozen or so babies, screaming, scrunched up, or sleeping, most with a shock of black hair and all with dark eyes looking like huge commas as they narrowed above the cheeks and towards the ears. I happened to look like an orangutan, swimming in a snowsuit four sizes too large, my cheeks pushed up towards round eyes, a crown of hair sticking straight up, as if someone had plugged my toe into an electrical outlet. My mom will quickly add that she loves orangutans—they are her favorite in the animal kingdom—so I can see how she'd want to bring me home.

I was part of the Korean diaspora, one of the thousands of children who were mostly cute, usually small, and always exotic in whatever country we landed. We grew up to become a generation of adults searching for connections to a land we called home, if but for a brief part of our lives. During the '70s, '80s and even '90s, we grew up in tiny towns and huge cities. Often we were the only Asians in a sea of white faces, whether it was in our class picture or at the family reunion. Our moms had blue eyes, and our dads were impossibly tall. We sounded just like our brothers and sisters, yet if you were to do a Sesame Street game of "One of these things is not like the others," invariably we'd be the ones who would stand out.

I never intended to travel to Korea; frankly, there were a hundred other places that better captured my imagination. But as a result of luck, coincidence, and circumstance, I had been invited on an all-expense paid tour of the motherland, and I figured: Go? Why the hell not! I'd never returned to the land where I was born, where I would look like everyone else, where I was supposed to have a connection to the people around me by virtue of a shared ethnicity and nationality. I set out to learn whether it is possible to have a homecoming in a place where there had never been a home.

Thirty-five years after leaving Korea, I returned for the first time. I gathered with 400 adult adoptees from around the world to share in the unique experience of coming "home" to Seoul for an international conference in August 2004. In previous years adoptees had grouped together in Washington, D.C., and Oslo, Norway, to share stories about searches for birth families, encounters with racism, and issues unique to the adoptee experience. This year's conference was different. Not only was this a reunion of friends who knew each other from the previous gatherings, but for all of us it was a reunion with our country, a land that many of us believed would hold secrets to our origins and a place to which some of us had thought we might never return.

I landed in Seoul with unbridled enthusiasm, eager to meet the Korean in me. I immediately tried the city's subway system, which was clean, efficient, and cheap, while striking out to shop in Itaewon, a neighborhood popular with tourists that is packed with tiny stores selling Korean souvenirs, leather coats, and designer purses. I lost myself in the maze of stalls and hordes of people in Namdemun, a huge outdoor market, with hundreds of merchants selling everything from ginseng to *hanboks* (traditional clothes) to jewelry to the Korean version of Tupperware. Tiny, wizened old ladies sat on pieces of cardboard selling chunks of ginger barely less gnarled than they were. Young men yelled at passersby to check out their products, a group of seniors marched through the market, and in the distance I could hear a voice chanting over a loudspeaker, like a bingo caller calling out numbers. The odors of kim chi and sweat permeated the air—a garlic and rotten cabbage stink—which pressed down upon me in the humid August air. But rather than feeling stifling, it was oddly comforting. And yet while immersed in Seoul, I felt no more embraced by my birth city than I had been by Tokyo, London, or Berlin during other trips.

Having done my share of international travel, it was not jet lag or culture shock that threw me; I was prepared for that. It was the surprising *lack* of connection I felt to this country. I had expected a feeling of returning to my past. But in order to have a homecoming, there needs to be a sense of what is home. I had not grown up with stories about the old country, celebrated *Chu Sok*, the harvest moon festival, or even seen movies featuring Seoul. Having been raised on a steady diet of *M*A*S*H*, this was not the Korea for which I had prepared myself. Korea had recovered from their great war and embraced the twenty-first century, complete with traffic, technology, and few remaining vestiges of the Hermit Kingdom it once was.

After a few days of exploring, it wasn't a place, but a person who made me feel as if I had returned to the beginning of my special story. Those of us at the conference sat through a number of meals featuring a multitude of distinguished guests making honorific speeches welcoming us home or, in some cases, apologizing that we had to leave at all. But it wasn't until Molly Holt was introduced that I felt a connection to Korea.

As a child I would pore over the *HI Families* magazine, published by the Holt adoption agency for families like mine. Each magazine would feature pictures of kids who looked exactly like me: Korean, but definitely Americanized in their dress, hobbies, and names. Many of the magazines would have pictures of Molly's mother Bertha, who lived and worked in Korea until her nineties, finishing a mission she and her husband had embarked upon in 1955 when they adopted and raised eight Korean children, along with their six biological children, while living in Oregon. Molly was in her late sixties, but she looked so much like her mother that I could mistake her for Grandma Holt, and I knew that she understood where I had been and where my story might lead upon my return.

While there, I learned *Arirang*, a Korean folk song, of which I have no conscious memory. The tune resonates inside me, recalls my past and threatens to invade my present. I didn't expect to discover a place where the smells, sounds, and even the music stir up long lost memories buried so deep that they weren't captured in my brain, but in my muscles. Will my present and my future involve Korea? For some returning adoptees, the trip was a new beginning, a return to home. As for me, I'm not sure if the trip was a step towards something, or the final chapter for this part of my life.

Of course, when 400 people come together for a common event, not all of them will have taken the same path. I was amazed at the vast variety of stories. I was born in 1967 and had been told that I was abandoned as an infant, nestled in a box placed on the steps of a Seoul police station. My first year was spent in an orphanage, where I contracted smallpox and became severely malnourished. Frail and tiny, I was placed in a foster home, where I spent a year before being adopted by my American family, just two days before my second birthday. Not an extraordinary story, but one that was well practiced and embellished with details like descriptions of the box I had called home for a few hours, or the showing of my smallpox scars. But my life, as far as I'm concerned, began in 1969 when I was handed to my parents in the San Francisco airport. I soon found my story tame compared to those of the people around me.

Here, I was meeting adoptees that really remembered Korea. I met two women who were adopted when they were teenagers. Each had maintained contact with her birth family and talked about siblings still in Korea. They understood many of the Korean customs and spoke the language. I was impressed: adoptees who could speak Korean! For them, a return to Korea was truly a homecoming in every sense of the word.

There are still adoption stories being written. While in Korea, I visited the Aeminwon Orphanage. Situated at the end of a long road in a rural suburb of Seoul, with its simple plastered buildings, dirt paths, and lack of playground or grass, it looks impoverished to the American eye. This orphanage has children from the ages of three to eighteen, but we were introduced mostly to the eight- to thirteen-year-old kids. I painted fans with a small group of children, and one of them reminded me of my seven-year-old daughter, with her shy nature, the way she ducked her head when I tried to talk to her, her huge almond-shaped eyes downcast through most of our meeting. My visceral reaction was to take her home: I wouldn't want my daughter to live here, so why let her stay? Two of the girls showed me their room, a concrete dormitory with no insulation, some peeling wallpaper, and scorch marks from a small fire, but spotless and well organized.

While they treated me to an impromptu piano recital, I tried to shake the sadness that I felt. I kept thinking over and over: I could have been one of them, but they could never be me. None of these children were available for adoption. Some were thought to be too old to adopt, some were disabled, but many were left by parents who had disappeared without signing the papers necessary to relinquish their rights, and so the children were stuck in legal limbo. Modern Koreans do not want to repeat previous tragedies where parents left their children at orphanages, intending to pick them up when times were better, only to return and find their children had been adopted and were continents away.

The reunion stories I heard while in Korea sent shivers down my back. "Did you hear?" someone next to me at dinner would ask, "She's meeting her birth parents today." Some of the adoptees came to Korea prepared to search for birth parents. They had visited the orphanages and agencies that handled their adoptions, and there were families who wanted to meet them. I was less organized, and frankly less motivated, the extent of which I didn't realize until sitting at a group banquet one evening.

A Korean woman came forward and through an interpreter, asked if one of us might be her daughter. For those of us with no idea who our birth mother could be, it was a sucker punch that knocked us into silence. As the interpreter announced the date of birth, I sat terrified and exhilarated, wondering how this moment would play out if it were on *Oprah*. My name could be announced as the winner, not just of a new car, but a new family. "You get a new family, and YOU get a new family!" Oprah would yell. No one there that night had that birthday, or maybe someone did and she chose not to step forward. All I know is that it wasn't me. I saw the mother's hope for a reunion spiral into loss as she was led crying out of the dining room, followed by TV cameras, and I exhaled in relief. I didn't want to be found, claimed, or picked up; a cosmic piece of lost baggage shuffling through the universe.

I look Korean, but when I opened my mouth in Seoul, I was immediately outed as a foreigner. Actually, I discovered I didn't even have to open my mouth; it hung around me, like an odor: my American clothes, my carriage, and my stance. One day, while shopping in a convenience store, I simply picked up a snack and paid for it, saying *kamsa hamnida* (thank you) as I left.

A Korean-speaking friend I was with followed me out saying, "Koreans are so nosy." "Why?" I'd asked. "Oh," she replied, "she knew you were not from here, and wanted to know what your story was." Here I was, halfway around the world, and a newfound friend was fielding questions similar to those that curious shopkeepers in Colorado had asked my parents: "Where is she from?" "Is she yours?" "What's her story?"

We were a great social experiment, babies and children, sent so far away from our birth land to live. It was an awkward awakening for me, learning that I felt more at home with my Anglo-American friend eating pizza in the Insadong neighborhood than when I was dressed up in my *hanbok*, pushing around the endless piles of kimchi on my plate. I sit in a state of limbo, racially Korean but culturally American, a puzzle piece that may be the right color, but doesn't fit any where, or perhaps a piece that fits perfectly, but it's a bold yellow in the midst of a blue sky.

Power of Adoption

Dominic Pangborn

Today I am flying to Redmond, Oregon.

I had never heard of this town until I read my ticket. It's not the destination I care about; it's the people I will meet. Looking back at my life, that's the way it's always been.

I was born in Korea in 1952—one year before the end of the Korean War. My father was an American soldier, fighting a war in a country that wasn't his own. My mother was a Korean farmer, forced to watch her homeland torn apart with violence and strife. In the midst of it, they somehow found each other, at least for one night. I don't believe he ever knew he had fathered a child—it was just one of those nights. However, as I see it, it was the best night; I was conceived.

My mother raised my three siblings and me. However, I was the only one with an American father. We grew up as simple peasants with little to nothing in our tiny village. Despite our humble surroundings, I loved that village. There was a sense of family and community that you only seem to find when you don't have much in the way of riches. In fact that sense of community shielded me from the name-calling and insults I'd later encounter when I started school in a neighboring village. It was in school where I started being identified as an "American bastard." The insults never bothered me, but I could tell it was different for my mother. She never said anything, but I felt her pain.

When I was ten, an opportunity presented itself in the form of America. Visiting American missionaries told my mother that they could bring me to America. However, I could only go by myself. She explained this to me and without hesitation I said yes. I knew the sacrifices that this would involve, but I saw the opportunity in front of me as well as the chance to spare my mother from any more pain.

I was put on a plane, and just like today I wasn't concerned where I'd end up, just that there would be somebody to meet me on the other side. I was told these people would be my new mother and father. I couldn't speak English, and they couldn't speak Korean, so we drove several hours in silence to their home in the Michigan countryside. This was my first ride ever in an automobile.

We arrived late at their house. There were already 11 children—from ages one to seventeen—lined up to greet me. I was overwhelmed by their hospitality. I thought, just like something that would've happened in my Korean village, the children of the community had come over to greet me. It wasn't until a week later, when none of them ever seemed to leave, that I realized that these were my new brothers and sisters. In fact, I realized I was no longer Jung Sung Hun. I had become Dominic Joseph Pangborn.

And I liked it.

I started school a short time later, still very unfamiliar with English. While my new brothers and sisters had been very welcoming, the other school children hadn't been as kind. On my first day one boy came nose-to-nose with me and called me a half-breed. I didn't understand the term right away, but I remembered hearing the week earlier in a cowboy movie called *Hombre*. Paul Newman played a half-Native American, half-Caucasian cowboy that's kicked and beaten by the other cowboys, all the while being called a half-breed.

The phrase suddenly clicked with me. As the boy continued to call me that, I stared him back down and simply said, "Yes, I am." He was stunned by my admittance. He expected me to be ashamed or embarrassed, but instead I wore it proudly. As I stared into his eyes, I realized our position had reversed. I saw the fear in his eyes and finally he turned and ran and ran. I knew now, it was not any different here from Korea.

I embraced my uniqueness. I was the only minority in an all-white community. There were no African Americans, Latinos, or Asians at all. In fact, I wouldn't meet another Asian until I went to college.

However, this didn't stop me from wanting to be a full American though. I quickly learned English as fast as I forgot the Korean. I played sports, but not just any sport, I played football. It was the most American sport I could play, and despite being undersized I was a part of the team. The football team. The Pangborn team. The American team.

For the most part the community came to accept me as one of their own. I never really felt any prejudice. If someone didn't like me, I always felt it was because of personal issues, not racial ones. I even dated quite a lot and never once heard a girl's parents say we couldn't date because of our racial differences.

It wasn't until I turned 15 that I actually met another minority. While working at McDonald's, I met Larry Hurd. Larry was the first black person I had ever met. He went to my high school and we felt a certain kinship in our minority status. Just like I had taken to the half-breed term, Larry had taken to one of his own.

"Call me J.B.," he'd say when introducing himself.

"J.B.?" someone would often ask.

"Yep, jungle bunny," he'd say with a laugh.

When his folks moved to Ohio, Larry would come live with the Pangborn family. Together we became the first Asian and first African-American to graduate from our high school.

After graduation, I moved to Chicago. There, I saw finally saw real diversity. However, it's also there where I really felt prejudice for the first time. I met an Italian girl from the once very Italian Cicero neighborhood. We'd had lunch, and I thought we should go on a date. She said that was impossible, and at first I didn't understand. I told her that I'd come over to her house, and she begged me never to try that, to not even think of it. I was confused at least until I saw the news that week. A black couple had moved into her little neighborhood and was literally chased out by an angry mob. The couple had to hide under their bed all night, waiting until daybreak to escape.

While that girl may have been a lost cause, that didn't stop me from celebrating the diversity of Chicago. I met so many new people, sampled so many different cultures, it was exhilarating. And to be honest I've never stopped celebrating that diversity even after I moved away from Chicago.

Today, I live in Michigan with my wife. And while the world knows me best as Dominic Pangborn, I'm still connected to my life as Jung Sung Hun. Like some adoptees do, I retraced my roots and was able to reconnect with my Korean siblings in adult life. When I returned to Korea some 20 years after I had left, I found my family. My mother had sadly passed away in that time, but the rest of my family was still there and they greeted me with open arms and we've remained close since. In fact, my two nieces—the daughters of my oldest brother—live with my family in Michigan. Today we are all one family from both sides of the ocean. Through the power of adoption, I didn't lose my Korean family—I gained an American one, too.

Color of My World...

Maria Wren

The color of my world changed within a single moment in time, and it remains an unforgettable stain in my memory. The experience of this first profound event dramatically influenced and defined the fabric of my life.

It began when I was the tender age of two. Instead of being in the typical "terrible two's," a different kind of terror was unfolded for me. Since that time, this incident remains vivid to me, coloring the view of my world, how I think and what I do.

I remember it well. At age two, it was a moment in time which I observed from the middle of a small, rectangular room. I can still see the satiny silk multicolored blankets of red, blue, yellow, and green on the floor. I can call to mind how the warmth of the sun felt as it filtered through the square, glass paned window; one that I recall was spotted with recent rain drops. The bright sunlight was a stark contrast to the scene unfolding before my myopic eyes, now blurred in tears. I couldn't talk well, but I recognized being torn apart by an emotional terror no two year old should ever feel.

I flinched when I heard the slapping punctuated by an anguished cry, which turned into a muted moan. There is a man, a tall man with his hands raised. One hand strikes down and hits the face of the woman who is now on her hands and knees. Knocked down, she is unable to get up, since the repetitious hits don't let her move.

With each slap she cries out. Then she mutes her sound as she meets my eyes. Her look is not filled with physical pain, rather one of agony, borne of helplessness and despair that seemed to penetrate her very soul. Watching, I hear the slash through the air before I see the strong hand meet with her head this time.

I cringe with each sound. I hear a thin, weak sound, cries of a child, bewildered and lost. Had that helplessness escaped from my mouth? I snap my gaze back at the man, and lock in on his black hair, intense dark eyes, and the shadowy hair on his arms. His tormenting image and his face are automatically recorded in my memory forevermore. It soaks in, becoming a permanent part of me. *Never to be forgotten.*

His gaze meets mine. He shouts something at me that I do not understand. But within me, I sense a sudden primitive, self-preserving fear and I press one tight hand against my mouth and cling tightly with the other around the soft, comforting blanket. The tension grew deep in my stomach, and I held my tiny fisted hand to my mouth to muffle the crying. It is an instinctive gesture. I am frozen in place, unable to break my eyes away from this frightening vision of events unfolding before me.

Later, I am warm and close to a body I know, and I am familiar with the touch and the scent. I recognize the soft sound of weeping while I rest on my mother's back, in the sling-like blanket, tied securely around her waist. I feel secure, but something deep within me is sad, profoundly sad, hearing the soft sound of despair in the agonizing sobs and in the sound of my mother's voice. Even at such a young age, I want to hold her, console her, and protect her from all harm. But I am a mere child, trapped in this body of a child. I'm too small to hold anyone, much less a body and soul too old for the vessel.

I cannot remember being an innocent, protected child. Childhood was not carefree. Instead it was colored gray and dark. I did not get to be a child! I felt old then and never felt the joy or the carefree innocence all children are supposed to experience. I aged that day and never went back. I lost childhood, lost the illusion that life is anything but what it was in that frightening moment and dark place in time that is embedded in my memory, and in my very being.

He is a bus driver. He is my mother's lover. She is his mistress. In Korea, she has no rights, no security, and no protection. And I follow in her footsteps and have nothing—only the sounds and visions that I cannot shut out.

It is my first childhood memory. The sounds of sobbing, of beating, of anguish and pain. I can't forget the experience of that moment no matter how I try. It is indelibly branded into my mind.

Time heals all wounds they say. I wish I could say that life was kind after that day, but it had other plans and other memorable experiences meant to give me character and eventually as a reminder of how God loved me. Today, I'm satisfied to know that He does not, and did not, allow more suffering than I could bear. The more He loves, the more trials He bestows on the loved one, to draw us closer to his greatness and plan.

I think that was just made up. I remember telling my adopted mom years later, I wish God would love me less.

They say each of us have a twin on earth somewhere. Years later, while watching TV in California, half a world away from Korea, I saw the "twin face" of the man who so many years ago had been branded into my memory. I was rooted immobile with all the dread and hatred in my teenage soul. Bile rose in my throat, my stomach knotted, and my fists tightened as if ready to strike out in rage.

It was the face of the tormentor, beater of a woman, my mother. But this man was an actor. His eyes were green not brown. But every other feature resembled HIM. I despised him on sight. The rational part of me knew this man to be a different man, an innocent one. But I will always remember HIM. I can never forgive men who resemble the image branded in my childhoods' memory.

I've learned that happiness is but fleeting moments to be grasped, captured, and savored. There are moments when I am lost in those past memories and relive the pain. Those moments are fleeting and I have grown with no expectation of life except what I can make of it.

The color of my world is dependent on my faith, my choices, and hope—and definitely this very moment in time! No one owes me anything; I am no more and I am no less than anyone. Life is what it is. And what matters is what we do with it from this very moment on. My face is turned forward, my eyes ready to reflect the color of my world, with faith in a good future yet to unfold.

Twilight

Becca Swick

I look at the sky in the midnight hour when everything is black.

Within the shadows beneath the stars, I can almost feel my past.

In the twilight just before sleep I can feel Omma's stroking my head.

A gentle singing of words barely heard. I fight the sleep.

I'm afraid to struggle. I don't want to scare her away.

Please give me more time with this precious gift before darkness comes to claim me.

Night gives away to a new dawn. I wonder does she dream this too.

From the Orphanage to Assimilation = Determination

Kim Lopez

Writing has been an utmost passion of mine as far back as I can remember. From my earliest days in America, I attribute this feeling to the five years of silence that I endured living in an orphanage in South Korea—unable to express my mind or voice my thoughts through language. That all changed when I was adopted and came to the United States at age six. Living in the United States, I immersed myself in speaking English while simultaneously adapting to a different culture. Each of these aspects was instrumental in defining and shaping the experiences which have made me the person I am today.

Learning to speak English was a challenge but an aspect of assimilation that I relished. After learning to speak my new language, I discovered my passion for writing. By expressing my thoughts and describing my memories, I was able to keep a vivid account of them. Writing itself was a powerful communication tool I could use to draw in my peers to experience how I felt. Particularly in English classes my peers and teachers would be enthralled by the images and descriptions that I'd invoke in my writing. Initially it was rather discomforting for me to be so personal about how I felt, but soon I came to realize that this was a gift that I could use to my advantage.

Writing has played a significant role not only to help me voice my thoughts, but has taught me the concept of determination. I endured numerous trials, one of which was being raised Korean-American in a racially prejudiced environment.

The death of my adoptive mother when I was twelve was an especially painful and difficult experience at a time when I was approaching puberty. I had grown attached to her and believed that she would be in my life for a long time. Therefore, I did not feel the need to express to her in words how I felt. I believed that such actions were unnecessary until it was too late. To this day, the memory leaves a bitter taste in my mouth and a profound regret for the unspoken words and the feelings I did not allow myself to express to her. Nonetheless, I overcame my pain while it strengthened my resolve to succeed in life despite the obstacles.

As I graduated from high school and branched out to life at the university, I evolved from a quiet, sheltered, awkward child to a confident individual and adult. My writing was a source of strength to me and provided comfort that I could turn to whenever I needed to express how I felt. I learned to speak out and describe the feelings that consumed me, mostly from my experience as a Korean-American, being an adopted child, and the loss of my adoptive mother. Added to that were the experiences that are part of the typical teenage angst. These experiences propelled me to turn to writing as a way of escaping from the harsh realities that I faced at times. They were also vital to me, not only mentally, but physically, and taught me determination in overcoming obstacles I would later encounter. People have been astonished by my ability to write so vividly and intuitively of my experiences. This has prompted me to realize my dream of writing as a career choice.

Three Cups

Rebekah Smith

In 1980 during my sophomore year of college, visits back home were still overwhelmingly depressing. For reasons I didn't know at the time, I once interrupted my rush to escape town that year with an impulse stop at the Korean grocery store. I hadn't gotten out much while living at home, so the store was still mysterious and intriguing.

The smell just inside the door, dry spice with a hint of dust, plus a hint of strong, fresh food, but not food I knew, altered my sense of place and familiarity instantly. Depression suddenly disappeared, replaced by pure curiosity of an exotic world to explore. Here were grocery store shelves, but not the familiar, readable ones I'd grown up with—the ones navigable quickly with an oblique glance from the end of the aisle ("Ah, yes, there's the soup"). These colors were recognizable, but were not the usual shades. Small boxes wrapped in plastic were mostly the same dimensions as our familiar boxes, but some were oddly flat enough, or engagingly square enough, to keep a sightseer cruising shelf after shelf.

There were clear packages and pictures that revealed their contents or invited guesses. These are grains of some kind. That's rice, of course. Here are desserts, seaweed, cookies, tea. The reward for discovery was simple, small, and pleasant. The lure of guessing was endless. Rainbows, pipes, teddy bears, and turtles inhabited the cookie section. And then, what was that flat, cream-white stuff? At the time I didn't know what dried squid looked like, and neither was there a picture of a squid on the package. I walked with quiet but transforming excitement, without the weight of knowledge and action. With no list, no dinner to cook, no prices to compare, with the same pleasure one can feel in warm, utterly foreign cafés where human voices are comforting but undemanding, their language incomprehensible.

In the drinks section with the coffee were a few boxes that looked very familiar in size. Labels had leaves and flowers, oranges, cups of brown liquid, even the word "Jasmine." The printed words must have said "Tea." Ah, the gold box with red and the picture of the ginseng root—that one was ginseng. It was the same red and gold as packages of ginseng gum. To an eight-year-old American's palate, the gum had tasted of sweetness, dust, and dirt and had taken a while to love. Once I was in college, "tea" meant expanding from Tetley's teabags to the romance of British Empire place names: Assam, Darjeeling, Irish Breakfast, English Breakfast, then to the moods and botanicals of health food stores, Sleepy Time, Morning Thunder, Peppermint, and (back to Empire) Mandarin Orange and Bengal Spice. Tea meant gentle, comforting tastes and someone who was glad to see you. We drank it from thick mugs in dorm rooms, from old china with the college matrons after church, from tin cups around campfires in the woods.

I had drunk it at home with Mom, in calm between the storms, when she was content for a while. She was predictable in those hours, and pleasant. The little crumbs of decent, mass-market tea, crushed, torn, curled, captive in a teabag, made a coffee-amber brew that caught the sunlight of the dining room and warmed our white, milk-glass mugs. We must have added honey. I remember the unavoidable stickiness dragging along the rim of the cups. Sometimes she served Constant Comment tea, flavored with orange and cinnamon that reminded us both of faraway, New York winters. We had been happy together then, too, at times. She had been a brave soul, a Southerner fighting isolation and the weight of a dark season with only the help of a bumptious, curious toddler. My body relaxes even now at those memories.

At the Korean grocery, suddenly, there was no relaxation. The man at the cash register said something in Korean. I answered in tense, embarrassed English. His face closed abruptly. He was probably a little surprised and a little embarrassed; I dropped into a large world of alarm and weird guilt. I remember this sensation, too: cold sweat, shallow breath, and confused thinking. He and I both stiffened into the expectant, vague, pretend-no-one-is-there posture of the self-conscious human in a crowd. Korean America and Korean-Adoptee America have shared this moment over and over. Is its accompanying flavor sweet ginseng? Bitter Tetley's?

Thirty years later, the South has mixed it up a little, and I have moved one state up and one state over to North Carolina. Now I visit "my" Korean grocery and take a regular grocery list. The women at the checkout there find no surprises in my usual basket of no-cook items and my delivery of a Korean community journal to their newspaper stand. We converse briefly at times. "I'm sorry, we do not make anymore. Mother is tired." "I like this brand a lot. It's almost as good as what you used to make." "Where is this from? It is free? You write it?" "Japanese student picnic. You can come." On very bad days I can still feel nervous. On medium and good days my body feels the permanent effect of time spent with 400 other Korean adoptees, years ago. What a sea of dark hair and eyes that must have been faces like mine, but striking me as foreign, of bodies like mine passing, jostling, standing in line, filling whole rooms. As in nature, as to the casual social eye, the similarity struck and sank in well before I met and knew individual people. Somewhere over the course of those days, an ancient dislocation inside my chest had eased and clicked into harmony like a broken bone set and instantly healed, like a stone column suddenly square on its base. It has stayed that way ever since.

I don't know whether there is a Japanese connection at my store, but aside from a few Korean herbals, the tea in their tiny tea section is a good, standard Japanese brand that includes powdered matcha and decent sencha, both of them the pure, simple, fresh, grass-greens that at grocery store prices may be gently boring but are never bad. Japan is serious about its tea. In a competitor Korean grocery 15 minutes away from mine, they don't know me well. They are reluctant to accept English language journals. They avoid Japanese brands. The tea shelf there is long, an earth-tone rainbow of herbals and blacks, all the equivalent of Tetley's or maybe even Twinings, not the place for a tea hound in search of traditional Korean tea. There is no whole-leaf green in the old style, no pounded, compressed set of small disks to be roasted and ground into powder. They did have one Korean powdered tea. I had to buy it, expensive though it was, although the dead-avocado green of its plastic bottle should have served as a warning. But who knew? Perhaps this was a type of Korean green tea I wasn't familiar with. In a world where even fine tea is crushed, fermented, flavored, crammed into bamboo tubes, or shaped like mushrooms, one must be willing to explore. Tea in a green ketchup bottle? Perhaps.

It was outstandingly awful. The pointed dispenser looked ideal for a fast, efficient squirt in a hurried, harried moment, the opposite of meditative tea ceremonies, so the office is where I experimented. Mid-afternoon, looking at the clock and then away from the glare of the computer, I sighed and let my spine straighten and shoulders and neck unclench. You can breathe deeply if you're not curled over like a grub and driven rigid with concentration. I climbed stiffly down the stairs to the lounge and heated some water. My aching wrists complained when I reached for my cup, inherited at the office from a friend long moved away. It was medium-thick porcelain, the size of a Western mug. Its white interior was ready to show off the color of tea just as my mother's milk glass once did. On the outside, orange and red flowers were outlined in gold, with graceful, strong lines on a field of blue leaves. The lighting in the office, a typical, head-splitting fluorescent, did nothing to enhance the tea. Even the cup could not help. The powder that woofed out of the tip of the bottle and into the water was lifeless, dusty, and greenish-grey. The taste of the mixture matched the color perfectly: bitter, chalky, and dead.

If you know what something is, and if that something is only so great, how can someone else claim it is marvelous and be believed? For most of us Americans, tea means sweet, dark iced tea, or a hot drink to sooth the throat, or a range of gentle, favorite herbals. It is strong, dark, and well doctored but never quite coffee, or it is middle class gentility in a parlor. "Oh, no, it's marvelous!" said a friend of the friend who had bequeathed me her office cup, "Chinese tea, that is. It is amazing. Intense, challenging, haunting, brilliant, rich with ancient tradition." I responded with a very reasonable, "How can it be?" His answer —so passionate about tea, so lovingly generous—came in the form of a long-distance, one-student course in fine teas. Boxes. Measures. Teapots. Cups. Information. Instructions. Tea. More tea. And as if they were a graduation gift, just before my 50th birthday he sent five small celadon cups that took my breath away. They were very simple—small, bell shaped, a celadon grey-green whose warm luminosity was simple yet intense. Staring at them was like staring into a quiet but living sea. Their maker was the artisan Haegang, reviver of the Koryo celadon tradition in modern Korea. Knowing nothing about pottery, I couldn't say whether or not it is consummate skill that makes a small cup nest into the hand as if it were alive and invites fingers to curl around it with a grace not their own. Surely the rim of a cup is just a rim, just ceramic or glass? But this bell curve set the lip to curve slightly and invited it to drink. The touch of cool ceramic on warm flesh was light but sensuous. How many objects can offer profound quietness and grace to the body, just with a touch?

Into this cup, shaped by Korean hands, made from Korean clay, goes tea from Hwagae Valley, a place I have never seen. It was made by Kim Shin Ho, a tea master central to the current revival of Korean tea tradition. In pictures online, his face and posture are very traditional; perhaps this is because of his ties to the Buddhist tradition. His hands can be seen in a brief video, tossing and rolling tea leaves in one of the many stages of its creation. He is countries away, but the sight of his face makes the word "tradition" a human reality—like the leaves of his tea, now here in my kitchen, whispery dry, slender, and curling delicately. I pick up a single leaf, not much longer than a rosemary leaf, and marvel. Korean air. Korean soil. The knowledge of how far it has traveled from its origin makes it powerfully exotic, though it is just a leaf. Like many teas, this one may taste better made from the water of its home country, the mineral of the water the same as the mineral of the soil it grew in. I won't know until I visit Korea. The dry leaf scent is nutty, with a hint of salt, but fresh like early spring and a fine day in autumn combined.

Hot water barely simmering, barely steaming poured at a slant pushes a small batch of the leaves around in an abrupt, dancing swirl. I am using a glass infuser, which is not at all traditional, but its glass sides turn ambient light into a golden glow, and this encloses yet shows off the leaves as they move in small currents. The gold grows gradually pale green as the tea infuses. From the infuser it is poured into a small pitcher, and from there into Haegang's teacup, the first tea the cup has ever held.

My hand is shaking. What claims and ideas have created this gut feeling that I have been separated all my life from what is my own? I haven't been. But the feeling is strong, and it responds to such simple things as shaped clay and a way of drying and toasting a leaf with a power that shocks me. Nothing but a cup, a sip of green tea—but a voice in my head says, "Welcome home." The taste is vegetal, verging on asparagus, with a freshness changing into a solid texture in the mouth. In this floats richness like nut flesh and a hint of toasted salt. There is a mild tang. After a swallow, the mouth texture change, and a mild sweetness, like a note of music sung high but soft, emerges from inside the fresh sensation and blooms, and then lingers. In the empty cup clings a fruit-like sweetness, pure as candy, addictive as a dear perfume.

"Be aware," said my tea mentor once, "of the *qi* brought to your body by the tea." The energy felt after drinking this tea warms my face and stomach. After infusing the leaves three more times, I am left with a sensation of mental lightness and clarity. This clarity does not extend to all that is meant by "home" or "mine," though in this instant, "mine" means a tiny moment of cultural tradition made solid in my hand and mouth. No one can challenge or replace it. It is not adopted, naturalized, bestowed by charity, in-lawed, step-parented, earned, feigned, bought, or permitted. "Home" of course is here in North Carolina. Korea is little but a distant travel plan. If Korea takes body and soul by surprise the same way this tea does, then it will not be bad that I've waited this long to go.

Prediction is useless, but who truly, ever, has no expectations? Empty the mind and the air that fills it will have a certain color, a certain scent much more delicate than tea. Korea will be a country, not a grocery store. Likeness and foreignness will be turned upside down, and then inside out. There will be no romantic distance; there will be unavoidable weight and bother. Or will romantic distance shimmer between me and the country forever? When I first traveled to Greece, a country I studied and taught for 26 years, I felt my interior life morph weirdly and turn into a solid old building in front of me. I could lean on it if I was tired. It was dry, rough, and hot from the sun. I could twist my ankle hiking over its ruins.

Of Korea, what is in my head? An alphabet, a few history books, the lunch menu, a few tea names, a great, deep, empty feeling of longing? But also today, a small green-grey part of it I hold in my hand, a taste and a lingering scent.

Authors and Artists

KATE AGATHON was adopted from Bangkok in 1978. She is a doctoral candidate in Curriculum Studies at Purdue University in West Lafayette, Indiana. A Colorado native, Kate enjoys hiking, mountain biking, and playing in the great outdoors.

DON GORDON BELL was on the first flight of Holt Adoption Program that left on May 21, 1956. Since 1995 he has lived in Seoul. He was a charter member of GOA'L, and is deep-

ly involved in adoptee issues with his blog *'Korean War Baby'* and on the current situation in *'This Thing of Ours—Adoption.'*

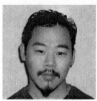

JOSIAH BELL was adopted from Seoul, South Korea, and grew up in Birmingham, Alabama, where he currently resides. He has established himself as an independent artist and is always working to educate people of the adoptee experience through his passion for art. "All my work is done with stencils and spray paint. I enjoy representing and validating the experiences, thoughts, and feelings of adoptees through my artwork."

KIM SUNDELL BROWN was adopted from Korea in 1956 and raised in Omaha, Nebraska. Kim and his wife, Lori, have two children (also adopt-

ed from Korea). He enjoys travel, sports, spending time with family, and advocating for children's rights. Kim is President & CEO of Holt International, and he says "When I am gone, I pray that one life will have been changed for the better because of my efforts."

MEGAN BROWN is finishing her bachelor of arts in telecommunications at the University of Kentucky in Lexington. Despite a disastrous first try, she has since learned to enjoy Korean food.

SARA CAMPION has a B.A. in music from Southeastern University in Lakeland, Florida. She currently resides in the Tampa Bay area where she teaches private music lessons.

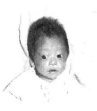 

Sara is active in her church and volunteers as a child advocate with Compassion International.

BRIAN CONYER currently resides in California and works as a medical sales representative. He has lived in Detroit, Raleigh, San Francisco, and now Los Angeles. Brian loves to travel and hopes to one day live in New York City before moving home to Raleigh to be close to his family.

KIM WOONGJEE De-GRAAF was adopted from South Korea in January 1985 by Dori and Rick DeGraaf. He grew up in Grand Rapids,

Michigan. Kim is currently residing in Phoenix, Arizona, after living in South Korea for the past 16 months. Kim's nickname "KimPab" is a reference to the food his adopted mom made for him when he first arrived in the United States.

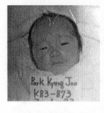 

KIRA DONNELL is a Korean adoptee poet, scholar, and advocate. In 2009, Kira reconnected with her birthmother after 27 years of separation. Kira was the first Korean adoptee to graduate from San Francisco State University's Asian American studies Master's program. Her thesis, "The Claiming of Identity, Agency, and Advocacy in Korean Adoptee Literature" explores common themes in poetry written by Korean adoptees. She currently works as the Youth Programs Coordinator at the Korean American Women Artists and Writers Association (KAWAWA), and is applying to PhD programs, where she hopes to research letters and poems written by Korean birthmothers.

JUDY ECKERLE was adopted to Minnesota from Korea at six months of age and works as an adoption professional. She's grateful to her family and friends for supporting her always and she continues to search for her birth family.

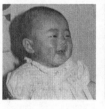 

ERIN ELLIS (Korean name Jee Hyun Jung) is a young woman with cerebral palsy. She uses a motorized wheelchair to get around and uses her mouth for day to day things like writing, drawing, typing, and eating. "I am a Holt adoptee, and very proud of it. Because of Holt, I am living life to the fullest. I enjoy art and poetry and aspire to be known one day for my art, but I am content helping others in whatever way I am able to. If I had not been adopted, I would never have become the person God wanted me to be, and would never have met the people who have helped me to grow. I am very blessed to lead a good life. I would rather have this disability and be the woman I am today, rather than be born with the ability to move but not know love and kindness. I am thankful to be loved and accepted for who I am."

JESSICA EMMETT was born and grew up in Hong Kong. Her birth parents were Vietnamese refugees who fled to Hong Kong after the Vietnam War. Jessica was adopted at the age  of one by a white British couple who were living in Hong Kong. At age 16, she moved to the United Kingdom, where she works as a freelance artist (www.jessica-emmett.com). Jessica is the founder of Adopted the Comic. Her work has been exhibited internationally. "I like to provoke thought and debate with my art rather than answer questions or judge adoption issues as right or wrong even if I do have my own opinions."

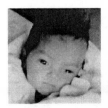 **KIMBERLY NEUMAN FAUNCE** (aka Kim Yong Hee) was adopted through the Holt International in February 1968. Ms. Faunce now lives in Fairfax, Virginia, with her husband and three children. Her youngest child also was adopted from Korea.

JENNY RYUN FOSTER has a Master's Degree in creative writing from the University of Hawaii. Her publishing credits include the book *Century of the Tiger* from the University of  Hawaii Press, 2003. *Century* won the Hawaii Book Publisher's award called the Ka Palapala Pookela for Excellence in Literature in 2004. Jenny's short fiction and non-fiction have appeared in various publications, including the *Korea Herald* and the *Hawaii Review*. She is a librarian and resides on the windward side of Oahu.

 **SANDRA GIBBONS** was adopted in 1977 from Seoul, Korea, at seven months old. She has a Bachelors degree in elementary education and currently lives in a suburb of Detroit, Michigan. She is a married mom of two amazing little guys (three and five) and happily stays home with them. Her mother is deceased, but her dad lives 2 miles away and they talk three times a day. "My parents have been my godsend and my saving grace. My husband is the best choice I've ever made. I've had an amazing life and have a long stretch of wonder ahead of me... Life's good"

CHERYL S. HAGEN is a member of The Church of Jesus Christ of Latter-day Saints and enjoys spending time with her family. When she isn't practicing percussion or clarinet, she  volunteers for various organizations in her community. She currently attends a private school in Oslo, Norway, to learn Korean and she can't seem to get enough of kimchi.

STEPHEN JOHNSON was born in Korea, adopted at four months, and grew up in Texas. He graduated from Baylor University with a BSW and Eastern University with an MA in international development. He now lives in Austin, Texas, where he will marry his soon-to-be wife.

KIM KING was adopted from Korea in 1973 at age eighteen months. She has her BFA from Syracuse University and MA from New York University. Kim is a founder of NJAAC/ New Jersey Adult Adoptee Community. She lives in Connecticut with her husband and two daughters. Kim blogs about crafts and adoption at 4crazykings.blogspot.com

DANIELLE KOEHLER is a twenty-seven-year-old, fun-loving girl who thought it would be quite interesting to write something about my story. "Not only for you but for myself also." She has two loving parents and two brothers and two sisters. "Love.Peace.Happiness.Hope.Faith is what really matters."

ANH ĐÀO KOLBE was born outside Sài Gòn, Việtnam and came to the United States via New York City in 1972. She left two years later and grew up with her Greek and German parents in Qatar and Oman. In April 2010, she returned to her motherland to document the reunion of forty-seven fellow Vietnamese

adoptees attending the first adult reunion hosted by Operation Reunite and Project Return II: Out of the Ashes. This collection of photographs and interviews is an ongoing series titled Misplaced Baggage: Same, Same But Different, to be published into a book and traveling exhibit.

Park Nam Sook, aka **KAREN LAIRAMORE PETTY**, is a graphic designer who married another graphic designer. "I guess you could say I really love art, design, and culture." Now she gets to stay home and watch her teenage kids, Adam and Parklynn, grow up. "Their lives have filled a huge void in my heart. Finally I am so grateful for life."

JOY LIEBERTHAL, LCSW, is a social worker and therapist in private practice in New York City and at the Juilliard Counseling Center. She was adopted from Korea at age six. She has lived in Korea and volunteered for a year at Orphans' Home of Korea in Uijongbu after undergraduate  school. Joy was one of the founders of the Korean Gathering in Washington, D.C., in 1999. She lives in New York with her husband and two boys.

KIM LOPEZ was born in Seoul, South Korea, and lived in an orphanage until the age of six when she was adopted by an American family. Growing up, she immersed herself in American culture but also dealt with being a Korean adoptee in rural Virginia. "I have learned to accept who I am, where I come from, and to be proud of my heritage as a Korean-American adoptee." Kim is a first-time mother of a little boy and lives in California with her husband, son, and two dogs.

MICHAEL MARCHESE lives in Madison, New Jersey, with his wife and two sons. He has a successful career in commercial real estate. Michael enjoys golfing and spending time with his family.

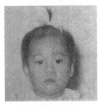

NANCY MCCULLOUGH, Canada's first foreign adoptee, resides in Pittsburgh, Pennsylvania, with her husband and two adopted daughters from China. Nancy is employed as a computer programmer/systems analyst and authored a book called *Adoption is for a Lifetime.*

ELIZABETH MEHAFFEY was adopted when she was three months old, and grew up in Oradell, New Jersey. Last spring, Liz lived in Seoul, where she taught English for Holt Ko-

rea. Liz has a strong passion for adoption, and has participated in various conferences and forums regarding adoption and foster-care. Liz is currently attending the University of Pennsylvania, where she is a graduate student, specializing in adoption counseling and policy. Liz enjoys photography, and some of her work has been featured in blogs and magazines.

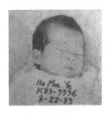

RENEE MEYER ERNST was born in Busan, South Korea, and adopted to the United States at age three months. Significantly influenced by her life as an adoptee, Renee's personal work explores notions of forming and expressing identity within cross-cultural contexts. Renee completed a Bachelor of Arts in studio art from the University of Northern Iowa, and a Master of Fine Arts in graphic design from Iowa State University. She is currently an Assistant Professor of graphic design at St. Ambrose University in Davenport, Iowa. Outside of teaching, Renee runs her own freelance design and photography business under the alias "Design by Mee" & "Mee Photography" (derived from her Korean name, Ha Mee Ye). She lives with her husband, Adam (also adopted from Korea) and enjoys spending quality time with their seven pets.

REBECCA MORRIS was born in South Korea and adopted at 18 months old. She grew up in Illinois and South Carolina and moved to California after high school. Rebecca has a Master's

degree in public health and is happily remarried with one child. She currently resides in California with her husband and four-year-old son. She aspires to be a world traveler and famous author someday.

KELSAY MYERS hails from Lowell, Michigan, and is currently an MFA candidate in creative writing at Saint Mary's College of California in Moraga, California. She has a fetish for wearing hats and enjoys reading philosophy to her Persian cat, Kierkegaard Mao.

DOMINIC PANGBORN is an acclaimed international artist/ designer. He lives in Michigan with his wife Delia and his two nieces from Korea.

JO RANKIN (Jung Im Hong) was born in Inchon in 1967, adopted by American parents in 1969, and raised in San Diego. She earned a journalism degree in 1989, then worked for two PBS stations. Jo Rankin (Jung Im Hong) co-founded the Association of Korean Adoptees (AKA-SoCal) in 1994 and co-edited *Seeds from a Silent Tree* (Amazon.com) in 1997. Jo and her husband live in San Francisco, where she also plays chess, duplicate bridge (life master), piano, and violin.

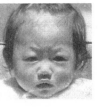

CHARLIE RITTS was adopted as Choe Soo-jung at 18 months in 1970 from Seoul to the mitten-shaped state of Michigan. Lisa "Charlie" Ritts bounced around from Chicago to New York to Paris before receiving her master's in Korean studies from the University of Washington. Currently, she lives on the North Shore of O'ahu and is writing a book with her mother about adoptive families. This poem, "It's Your Choice," was written during a particularly dark period in the author's not-too-recent past; for numerous other adoptees, these dark periods are far too often and frequent.

KEVIN RIUTZEL currently lives in San Diego, California. He works for emergency and non-emergency ambulances in multiple facets while studying to pursue a career in medicine. Kevin has spoken at Asian-American leadership conferences as well as to parent groups from the perspective of someone who was internationally adopted. He has been to Korea three times and plans to visit again in the near future. Kevin likes all types of food and chillaxin' with friends.

BETSY SCHAFFER was adopted in 1970 at age three from Seoul, Korea. She has lived in Japan, Virginia, Oklahoma, and California with her adoptive  family. She now writes poetry to help express the myriad of emotions that come with such an experience. Betsy currently lives in Santa Barbara, California, with her husband and cat, Betsy, where she is a CPA and helps manage software development projects. She enjoys reading, writing, and hanging out with other adoptees.

 **CHANDRA SCOTT** grew up in the beautiful state of Montana and now lives in North Carolina. She and her husband, Charlie, have been married for 20 years and have 3 wonderful boys—Caleb, Christian, and Calvin.

After an early start in upstate New York, **REBEKAH SMITH** has lived in Alabama, Tennessee, Georgia, and North Carolina. She has just retired from teaching college Greek  and Latin and spends time in reading, writing, tea drinking, Argentine tango, yoga, housework, and the care and sailing of an old wooden boat.

JENNIFER SNYDER (Song Jin Yung) was born in Korea and adopted in 1975 before she was a year old. She was raised in Minnesota where she still lives today. Jennifer works in finance at the University of Minnesota. She has not yet returned to Korea but looks forward to doing so in the near future.

KATE SULLIVAN was born in Pusan and adopted as an infant by a family from the United States. She grew up in Connecticut and New Hampshire as one of five children (three others also adopted from Korea). She attended Trinity College and Yale University and currently lives just outside New York City with her husband and cat.

SUZANNE SWANSON was born in rural Kyong-gi Province in South Korea. She came to the United States in 1984 and has lived in Nebraska all her life. Her hobbies include photography, being an expert on Scooby-Doo trivia (and obsessed with Scooby-Doo), singing, playing the flute, reading and scrapbooking when she has time. Suzanne has two Bachelor's degrees: one in liberal arts with an emphasis in human relations and psychology and a Bachelor of Arts in human relations. She currently works with adolescent males who have been adjudicated by the court to residential treatment for chemical dependency.

BECCA SWICK was born in Busan in 1961. She was adopted in 1964 and raised in New Jersey. Becca is one of nine authors of "Once They Hear My Name." She describes herself as  "on the ever-evolving road of a Korean American Adoptee."

 **KAYLA TANGE** was born in Seoul and adopted by a Japanese-American family at the age of six months. She and her adopted sister were raised in a small agricultural town in Central California. Kayla is a performance artist and fashion designer with a love for photography. She developed a book project with friend Bruce Malone. "The idea began when we met at one of my performances and I told him my story of adoption—how I have been on a journey to put the pieces together and express my feeling of confusion, loss, belonging, and identity. The book touches on the important issue of identity, which I know many adoptees have experienced at some point in their life—myself included."

SUSAN TIEDEMANN was adopted from Korea in 1983. She currently works as an attorney in Washington, D.C., and has a strong interest in international adoption law.

 **MARY LEE (HOEFT) VANCE** (aka Lee Myung Ja) arrived in Wisconsin in 1961. She earned her Ph.D. from Michigan State University in higher education administra-

tion in 1993 while working full-time. Mary Lee has worked in higher education student services since 1984 in a variety of capacities. She has taught both undergraduate and graduate courses, edited two books, published in refereed journals, and presents internationally on a wide variety of topics. Mary Lee is currently at the University of Montana where she is the Director of Disability Services. She is a polio survivor, enjoys hand cycling and sled hockey and in her spare time writes book reviews and food articles for *Korean Quarterly*, and of course loves eating.

PETER EUGENE VIN-YARD, a.k.a. 서인주, was adopted from Korea at the age of 3, to the Vinyard family, in Oregon. He currently resides in Sacramento, California, and

sits on the board of directors for also known as (AKA-SF). In 2010, Peter was reunited with his birth family and continues his journey through writing and being involved in the adoption community.

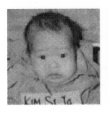

LOEY WERKING WELLS has lived in Portland, Oregon, since 1993, but considers the world her playground. When she isn't writing, volunteering, or driving her daughter Dylan around, she is masterminding her family's next adventure.

MARIA WREN was adopted in 1967 at age eleven. "I am Amerasian and being an older child at adoption, the memories of discrimination experiences are vivid. However, I never felt

any animosities or resentments. It was what it was." Maria lives in San Francisco and looks forward to new opportunities and a trip to Korea next year.

COURTNEY YOUNG was adopted from Korea in 1988. She graduated from the University of Oregon in the School of Journalism and Communication. Courtney lives in Eugene, Oregon, and works for Holt International.

Acknowledgements

More Voices: A Collection of Works from Asian Adoptees was published in celebration of Holt International's fifty-fifth anniversary and as part of the International Forum in Washington, D.C., in April 2011. The event was hosted by Holt International and Adoptees for Children.

I am grateful to the dedicated individuals who brought this book from an idea to completion: Courtney Rader and Courtney Young, who organized the submissions and managed the multiple details of approvals, photos, and biographies of the selected authors and artists; Mary Lee Vance for her help in finalizing selections; and Michelle Nicolson for putting it all together and still smiling through "one more thing."

My grateful appreciation to each of the artists and authors who contributed to this book—their only compensation was the satisfaction of being a part of this project. This collection of work represents incredibly private, sometimes raw, and deeply personal life experiences. For the reader their contributions will inspire and provide new insights into the complex world of intercountry adoption through the voices of those who live it. *More Voices* includes contributions from adult adoptees representing a variety of countries and reflects their varied experiences as individual adoptees.

Most of all, we acknowledge Brian Boyd and Yeong & Yeong Book Company. His unwavering support, dedication and commitment to birth mothers and adult adoptees is beyond measure and brought *More Voices: A Collection of Works from Asian Adoptees* to reality. A portion of the proceeds from the sale of *More Voices: A Collection of Works from Asian Adoptees* will benefit the lives of children whose voices have yet to be heard.

CPSIA information can be obtained
at www.ICGtesting.com
Printed in the USA
LVOW11s0100110917

548250LV00001B/285/P